THE MAGUS OF THE NORTH

Johann Georg Hamann (1730–1788) in 1785

THE MAGUS
OF THE NORTH

*J. G. Hamann and the Origins of
Modern Irrationalism*

ISAIAH BERLIN

Edited by
Henry Hardy

FARRAR, STRAUS AND GIROUX
NEW YORK

First published in 1993 by John Murray (Publishers) Ltd., 50 Albermarle
Street, London W1X 4BD, United Kingdom
First American edition, 1994
Frontispiece: Johann Georg Hamann in an engraving of 1785
signed "Fleischmann," probably copied from the portrait
by a "Mlle Podbielski" referred to by Hamann in a letter to F. H. Jacobi,
3 December 1785. Reproduced from D. E. Kühn, *Johann Georg Hamann, der
Magus im Norden* (Gütersloh, 1908)

Library of Congress Cataloging-in-Publication Data
Berlin, Isaiah, Sir.
The magus of the north : J. G. Hamann and the origins of modern
irrationalism / Isaiah Berlin ; edited by Henry Hardy.
p.   cm.
Originally published: London : J. Murray, 1993.
Includes bibliographical references and index.
1. Hamann, Johann Georg, 1730–1788.   2. Irrationalism
(Philosophy)—History—18th century.   I. Hardy, Henry.   II. Title.
B2993.B47   1994   193—dc20   93-37639   CIP

For Henry Hardy

CONTENTS

EDITOR'S PREFACE

ISAIAH BERLIN'S first publication about Hamann appeared in 1956, in the form of a chapter in his selection from the eighteenth-century philosophers.[1] Thereafter he has discussed Hamann in some of his essays,[2] but has not treated him in any published work in the depth one might have expected, given the central position Hamann's ideas have undoubtedly occupied in his study of intellectual history. I had thought of this disappointing lack as irremediable until I encountered a collection of draft material dating from the 1960s, which, taken together, clearly represented the greater part of a much more detailed study of Hamann's ideas. So thoroughly had Berlin dismissed this material from his mind that, until I found it, he assured me that nothing of the kind existed. It did, and this book is based upon it.

The stimulus for the composition of the drafts was an invitation to deliver the Woodbridge Lectures at Columbia University in New York in 1965. The title given to the lectures was 'Two Enemies of the Enlightenment'; the other enemy was Joseph de Maistre. The original plan was to publish a revised version of the typescripts on which the lectures were based, but although Berlin did a certain

[1] *The Age of Enlightenment: The Eighteenth-Century Philosophers* (Boston and New York, 1956; Oxford, 1979), pp. 270–5.

[2] Least briefly in 'The Counter-Enlightenment' (1973) and 'Hume and the Sources of German Anti-Rationalism' (1977), both reprinted in *Against the Current: Essays in the History of Ideas* (London, 1979; New York, 1980). See also *Vico and Herder: Two Studies in the History of Ideas* (London and New York, 1976).

amount of further work after the lectures were delivered, he remained dissatisfied with what he had written, and the drafts were laid aside. Twenty-five years later the material on Maistre was rescued, in the form of a long essay in Berlin's most recent collection;[1] Hamann has had to wait a little longer.

Something should be said about the establishment of the text, if only as a necessary background to the expression of my many debts of gratitude. Collation of the surviving typescripts revealed a substantial and crucial gap (of several pages, it turns out) at the end of the chapter on language. Without this missing material, publication would scarcely have been practicable. By a happy accident some of the dictated recordings on which the drafts were based had not been discarded; but they were made on 'Dictabelts', a technology long superseded, so that they seemed, at first, to be indecipherable. However, with the aid of the National Sound Archive, an example of the relevant machine was found in London's Science Museum. Once this had been put in working order, it was possible to transfer to modern cassettes the sound preserved on the Dictabelts. Miraculously, as it seemed at the time, the surviving recordings did include the missing pages of the text; indeed, they also provided further passages whose absence would not otherwise have been apparent. I pay tribute to Benet Bergonzi, Timothy Day and their colleagues at the National Sound Archive for their unfailing helpfulness and their technical expertise, without which this book could not have appeared in its present form, if at all.

Up to the point at which this gap occurred, the book is principally based on a largely continuous draft typescript. The remainder of the text was represented by a number of

---

[1] 'Joseph de Maistre and the Origins of Fascism', in *The Crooked Timber of Humanity: Chapters in the History of Ideas* (London, 1990; New York, 1991).

discontinuous passages of varying length, not all of which had been assigned a definite position in the overall structure; it is clear that they were destined for incorporation, but the project was abandoned before the final synthesis was performed. My aim in grafting these passages on to the main typescript has been to assemble, so far as I could manage, a readable text in which topics are discussed in a natural order: I trust that any remaining seams and imperfections are not too obtrusive. Isaiah Berlin has kindly read through the result, approved it, and improved it enormously;[1] to revisit and revise a somewhat disjointed draft laid aside decades previously is a deeply unappealing task, and I am extremely grateful to him for his willingness to undertake it.

My other principal concern has been to trace, check and provide references for as many as possible of the numerous quotations which the text contains.[2] This work, which has led me down some unexpected and occasionally unfrequented byways, could not have been completed without the help of a number of scholars, to whom I should like to express my thanks. Professor James C. O'Flaherty, the leading expert on Hamann in the English-speaking world, has given of his time and knowledge in abundance, with unstinting generosity, when he has been hard pressed by other preoccupations: it is no exaggeration to say that his

---

[1] The text has not been revised in any systematic way to take full account of more recent work on Hamann, which in any case does not invalidate its central theses.

[2] Berlin's notes, where they survive, frequently contain the necessary clues, but other notes seem to have disappeared. Hamann scholars may like to know that one important source, not usually mentioned in Hamann bibliographies, was V. A. Kozhevnikov, *Filosofia chustva i very v eya otnosheniyakh k literature i razionalizmu XVIII veka i k kriticheskoi filosofii* [The Philosophy of Feeling and Faith in its Relations to the Literature and Rationalism of the Eighteenth Century and to Critical Philosophy], vol. 1 (Moscow, 1897), which contains a very extensive treatment of Hamann.

help has been indispensable, and my gratitude to him is proportionate.[1] Professor Renate Knoll's remarkable store of information about Hamann and his world enabled her to solve for me several problems that might otherwise have proved intractable. Roger Hausheer has, with unflagging patience, put his knowledge of German and of the history of ideas at my disposal on innumerable occasions, to the great benefit of the book. Patrick Gardiner has read more than one draft of the text and enabled me to make a number of significant improvements. I have received help on individual points from Professor Frederick Barnard, Gunnar Beck, Dr Julie Curtis, Dr Anne Hardy, Veronica Hausheer, Professor Arthur Henkel, Dr Leofranc Holford-Strevens, Dr Aileen Kelly, Professor Ze'ev Levy, Professor T. J. Reed, Dr John Walker and Dr Robert Wokler. And I have been assisted, sometimes well beyond the call of duty, by many librarians: most directly in the line of fire in Oxford have been Adrian Hale, Librarian of Wolfson College, and the staffs of the Bodleian Library and the Taylor Institution Library.

I have three more general sources of benefaction to mention. In the first place, it is a pleasure to acknowledge the very generous support of three charitable foundations, without whose help it would have been impossible to undertake the larger project of which this volume represents a first instalment. Next, I must confess that I can find no words adequate to describe the practical or psychological importance of the assistance provided by Pat Utechin, the author's secretary. Finally, Lord Bullock knows that I tell the truth when I say that it is only through his original

---

[1] Professor O'Flaherty has not only helped in the search for sources, but has thrown light on numerous matters of substance. It should not therefore be assumed, of course, that he is in agreement with the author's judgements. Isaiah Berlin takes sole responsibility for what is said in the book.

intervention on my behalf that I have been in a position to incur any of the other obligations mentioned above.

Wolfson College, Oxford   HENRY HARDY
April 1993

Postscript

After the first impression of the UK edition of this book had been printed, Chapters 1, 2 (to page 18) and 7 were published in the *New York Review of Books*, 21 October 1993, pp. 64–71. A number of minor changes were made by the author in this connection, and I have now incorporated most of these in the book. At the same time I have taken the opportunity of eliminating a handful of slips and infelicities that had come to light since the book went to press, and I should like to thank those who brought them to my attention. I should also like to take this opportunity of thanking – belatedly – Hugo Brunner, Gail Pirkis and their colleagues at John Murray for the patience and professionalism with which they have withstood my particularity.

October 1993

AUTHOR'S PREFACE

THE FAMOUS PHRASE 'God-intoxicated man' fits Hamann far better than the wildly romanticised Spinoza of the eighteenth-century German critics. For Hamann everything – all there is and all that could be – is not only created by God, and serves his inscrutable purposes, but speaks to us, his creatures, made in his image. Everything is revelation. Everything is a miracle. Causality is illusory. All that is created by God's will reveals reality, truth, speaks to those who have the eyes and ears to grasp it. *Te saxa loquuntur*; but not only stones and rocks speak the Lord, everything does: in the first place, of course, Holy Writ, and the words of the saints and the fathers and the doctors of the Christian Church, and of their forerunners in Judaea and Greece, and its dissident child, Islam. But in addition to this the whole of history, facts, events, all that human beings are, think, feel, do – and not only human beings: nature, fauna and flora, earth and sky, mountains and streams, and all natural events – speak to us directly; are the form and substance of the language in which God implants knowledge in us.

But Hamann is clear that we can receive it only if we can read this language – if its meaning is revealed to us – and that may well vary between individuals and societies. It is obfuscated by those who mistakenly believe that what matters are the inventions and creations of men, of individuals – the arts and the sciences, and above all theories, systems, artificial creations which deaden the living life of the universe in its continuous activity. Spontaneity is everything: imaginative intuition, not the logic and classifications and systems of the theorists, opens the windows through which the divine light comes to us. All that we are and do and make – including the arts and the sciences and the means by which we live our ordinary lives – has no meaning save as the expression of God's communication to us; all that there is – animate and inanimate – forms a single seamless whole. We cannot see it all, for we are finite beings, and can only see parts, fragments, but that is sufficient to give us understanding; understanding, not the knowledge of the experts, the scientists, those who arrange and order and collect and distribute and build systems. Goethe says somewhere that the living butterfly, with its bright, beautiful colours, once it is pinned down by Moses Mendelssohn turns into a grey lifeless corpse; so Hamann too contrasts the intuitive insight, the imaginative grasp of reality with the lifeless material of the systematisers and the dissecters. That is the heart of his theory of cognition, experience, being and the world. No generalities, only the particular is real. Direct revelation, not analysis – that is the heart of his vision.

But I must own that Hamann's vision is not the subject of this essay: Hamann's theology and his religious metaphysics I find I am neither drawn to nor competent to discuss, except in so far as they are part and parcel of the rest of what he wrote. This has been done very well by others. My interest lies in the fact that Hamann is the first out-and-out opponent of the French Enlightenment of his time. His attacks upon it are more uncompromising, and in some respects sharper and more revealing of its shortcomings, than those of later critics. He is deeply biased, prejudiced, one-sided; profoundly sincere, serious, original; and the true founder of a polemical anti-rationalist tradition which in the course of time has done much, for good and (mostly) ill, to shape the thought and art and feeling of the West. I do not speak as a champion of Hamann's views, only as a witness of a great deal that is truly revealing in the scattered, unsystematic, passionate, and always deeply committed writings of this eccentric thinker – one of the important if often maddening irregulars of civilisation.

March 1993   ISAIAH BERLIN

1   INTRODUCTION

Do either nothing or everything; the mediocre,
the moderate, is repellent to me: I prefer an extreme.

Hamann to J. G. Lindner, 20 May 1756[1]

Think less and live more.

Hamann to J. G. Herder, 18 May 1765[2]

THE MOST passionate, consistent, extreme and implacable
enemy of the Enlightenment and, in particular, of all forms
of rationalism of his time (he lived and died in the eighteenth century) was Johann Georg Hamann. His influence,
direct and indirect, upon the romantic revolt against universalism and scientific method in any guise was considerable
and perhaps crucial.

This may seem at first sight to be an absurd claim on
behalf of a man whose name is scarcely known in the English-speaking world, who is barely mentioned, at best, in
some of our larger or more specialised encyclopaedias as an
esoteric writer, confused and obscure to the point of total

---

[1] References to Hamann's writings are to Johann Georg Hamann,
Sämtliche Werke, ed. Joseph Nadler (Vienna, 1949–57) (hereafter W), and
Johann Georg Hamann, *Briefwechsel*, ed. Walther Ziesemer and Arthur
Henkel (Wiesbaden and Frankfurt, 1955–79) (hereafter B), by volume,
page and first line, thus: B i 202.2 (the reference for this first epigraph).
[2] B ii 330.30.

unintelligibility, an eccentric and isolated figure, about whose views – beyond the fact that he was consumed by some kind of highly individual Christianity, usually described as a form of pietism, believed in the occult truths of divine revelation and the literal inspiration of the Bible, rejected the French atheism and materialism of his time, and was at most a minor figure in the German literary movement known as *Sturm und Drang* ('Storm and Stress') – virtually nothing is said. Literary histories and monographs sometimes speak of him as a minor contributor to the turbulence of the 'pre-romantic' German literature of the 1760s and 1770s; he occurs in the biographies of Kant as a fellow citizen of Königsberg, as being an unhappy dilettante, an amateur philosopher whom Kant once helped, then abandoned, and who criticised Kant without understanding him; and biographies of Goethe occasionally contain a few admiring quotations about him from Goethe's autobiography, *Dichtung und Wahrheit*.

But no definite impression emerges: Hamann remains in these histories (as he did in his life) in the margin of the central movement of ideas, an object of mild astonishment, of some interest to historians of Protestant theology, or, more often, altogether unnoticed. Yet Herder, whose part in altering historical and sociological writing can hardly be disputed, once wrote to him that he was content to be 'a Turkish camel-driver gathering up sacred apples before his ambling holy beast, which bears the Koran'.[1] Herder revered Hamann as a man of genius, looked upon him as the greatest of his teachers, and after his death venerated his ashes as the remains of a prophet. America was indeed called after Amerigo Vespucci, but it was Columbus who discovered that great continent, and in this case the Columbus, as Herder freely admitted, was Hamann.[2]

[1] B ii 315.35.
[2] Goethe saw Hamann as a great awakener, the first champion of the unity of man – the union of all his faculties, mental, emotional,

Hamann's disciple F. H. Jacobi transmitted much of his thought to the romantic metaphysicians of the beginning of the nineteenth century. Schelling regarded him as a 'great writer' whom Jacobi perhaps did not understand at all;[1] Niebuhr speaks of his 'demonic nature' and its superhuman strength;[2] Jean Paul says that 'the great Hamann is a deep heaven full of telescopic stars and many nebulae that no human eye can resolve',[3] and even for a romantic writer goes to unheard-of lengths to praise his unique, unsurpassed genius; in the same spirit Lavater says that he is content to 'collect the golden crumbs from his table',[4] and similarly Friedrich Karl von Moser, 'the German Burke', admires his eagle flight.[5] Even if some of this is due to the enthusiasm of contemporaries which left little trace on later generations, it is still sufficient to stir curiosity about the character of this peculiar figure, half hidden by the fame of his disciples.

Hamann repays study: he is one of the few wholly original

---

physical, in his greatest creations – man misunderstood and misrepresented, and indeed done harm, by the dissection of his activity by lifeless French criticism. In book 12 of *Dichtung und Wahrheit* he expresses Hamann's central principle thus: 'Whatever a man wants to accomplish – by deed or word . . . – must have as its source his united powers in their totality, since all that is divided is worthless.' (See Goethe, *Aus meinem Leben: Dichtung und Wahrheit*, ed. Siegfried Scheibe, vol. 1 (Berlin, 1970), pp. 424–7, quotation at p. 426, line 7.) Goethe wrote to Frau von Stein about his delight in grasping more of Hamann's meaning than most men. *Goethes Liebesbriefe an Frau von Stein 1776 bis 1789*, ed. Heinrich Düntzer (Leipzig, 1886), p. 515 (letter of 17 September 1784).

[1] *F. W. J. Schelling's Denkmal der Schrift von den göttlichen Dingen etc. des Herrn Friedrich Heinrich Jacobi . . .* (Tübingen, 1812), p. 192.

[2] *Lebensnachrichten über Barthold Georg Niebuhr aus Briefen desselben und aus Erinnerungen einiger seiner nächsten Freunde* (Hamburg, 1838), vol. 2, p. 482.

[3] Jean Paul, *Vorschule der Ästhetik*, part 1, § 14: p. 64 in Norbert Miller's edition (Munich, 1963).

[4] *Friedrich Heinrich Jacobi's auserlesener Briefwechsel* (ed. Friedrich Roth), vol. 1 (Leipzig, 1825), p. 438.

[5] B ii 230.9.

critics of modern times. Without any known debt to anyone else, he attacks the entire prevailing orthodoxy with weapons some of which are obsolete and some ineffective or absurd; but there is enough force in them to hamper the enemy's advance, to attract allies to his own reactionary banner, and to begin – so far as anyone may be said to have done so – the secular resistance to the eighteenth-century march of enlightenment and reason, the resistance which in time culminated in romanticism, obscurantism and political reaction, in a great, deeply influential renewal of artistic forms, and, in the end, in permanent damage to the social and political lives of men. Such a figure surely demands some degree of attention.

Hamann is the pioneer of anti-rationalism in every sphere. Neither of his contemporaries Rousseau and Burke can justly be called this, for Rousseau's explicitly political ideas are classical in their rationalism, while Burke appeals to the calm good sense of reflective men, even if he denounces theories founded on abstractions. Hamann would have none of this: wherever the hydra of reason, theory, generalisation rears one of its many hideous heads, he strikes. He provided an arsenal from which more moderate romantics – Herder, even such cool heads as the young Goethe, even Hegel, who wrote a long and not too friendly review of his works, even the level-headed Humboldt and his fellow liberals – drew some of their most effective weapons. He is the forgotten source of a movement that in the end engulfed the whole of European culture.

2 LIFE

HAMANN'S LIFE, at any rate in its outward aspects, was uneventful. He was born on 27 August 1730 in the East Prussian capital of Königsberg.[1] His father, Johann Christoph, came from Lusatia and was apparently a surgeon barber who became the supervisor of the municipal bath-house, a fact in which he took some pride. His mother, Maria Magdalena, came from Lübeck. His social origins were therefore not very different from those of Kant and Schiller, and a good deal more humble than those of Goethe, Hegel, Hölderlin and Schelling, not to speak of the sons of the gentry and the nobility. The background of the family was pietist; that is to say, it belonged to, although it was not at all prominent in, that wing of German Lutheranism which, inspired by the revolt against book learning and intellectualism generally that broke out in Germany towards the end of the seventeenth century, laid stress on the depth and sincerity of personal faith and direct union with God, achieved by scrupulous self-examination, passionate, intensely introspective religious feeling, and concentrated self-absorption and prayer, whereby the sinful, corrupt self was humbled and the soul left open to the blessing of divine, unmerited grace.

This highly subjective wing of German Protestantism had its analogues in the Moravian Brotherhood, in the mysticism of Jakob Böhme's English disciples (Pordage,

---

[1] Today part of the Russian Federation, and officially known since 1946 as Kaliningrad.

for example), of Weigel, Arndt, and the followers in the eighteenth century of William Law, of the Methodist preachers – the Wesleys and Whitefield – and of Swedenborg and his disciples, among them William Blake. It spread widely in Scandinavia, England and America, and in some of the Masonic and Rosicrucian lodges both in France and in Germany. The German pietists were distinguished by a personal emotionalism and, in the second half of the century especially, a gloomy puritanical self-abasement and self-mortification, and a stern opposition to the pleasures of the world and especially the secular arts,[1] for which the Calvinists of Geneva, Scotland and New England had also been known.

Even if the ascetic and introspective quality of this outlook can be traced in Hamann's character and views, the bleak puritanism, of which there are notable traces in Kant – a child of a similar environment – is wholly absent. So too is the shallow and sometimes hysterical emotionalism of some pietist confessional writing. Hamann appears equally free both from the narrow hatred of learning which caused the expulsion of Leibniz's disciple, the philosopher Wolff, from Halle earlier in the century, and from the more exhibitionist forms of German Protestantism, though he did remain devoted to Luther's life and personality to the end of his days.

His education was somewhat desultory. He was instructed by a former priest who believed in teaching Latin without grammar. He and his brother wandered from one small and sordid school to another and never acquired respect for system of any kind. By the time he reached fifteen, the normal age for higher education in Germany at that time, he managed to scrape into Königsberg University, where he heard lectures on history, geography, philo-

---

[1] See the interesting account in *Anton Reiser*, the well-known novel by Goethe's admirer Karl Philipp Moritz.

sophy, mathematics, theology and Hebrew, and displayed considerable gifts. He listened to the philosophical lectures of Knutzen, who had also taught Kant, and took some interest in astronomy and botany. He did not seem to be drawn to theology. He preferred, he tells us in his autobiography,[1] 'antiquities, criticism . . . poetry, novels, philology, French authors with their peculiar gift for invention, description, and capacity for giving delight to the imagination'.[2] He deliberately evaded acquiring useful knowledge and obstinately pursued humane studies for their own sake, determined to remain a servant of the Muses.[3]

He lingered on for six years at the University, took part in student literary publications, made friends, and is described as a man of passionate, affectionate and sensitive character, frank and impulsive, with a quick temper, in need of affection, timid, high-minded, with fastidious literary taste. His writings of that period are of no great interest. His style had not developed the eccentric attributes for which it – and he – became notorious in later years. At the age of twenty, in the literary periodical *Daphne*, he appears as a typical young German of the *Aufklärung*, uttering impeccably conventional sentiments derived from the fashionable French writers, with a tendency, not uncommon in German writers of that time, towards a heavy-footed style, an effort to imitate Gallic *esprit* and gaiety which in the German imitators often becomes clumsy, elephantine, embarrassing and pathetically lacking in wit. He read enormously and chaotically and began that vast accumulation of apparently unrelated information which cluttered his pages in later years.

After the University he was not sure what career to choose: he was regarded as a promising young littérateur, a disciple of the French *lumières*, who might make his mark

---

[1] *Gedanken über meinen Lebenslauf* (W ii 9–54).
[2] W ii 21.3.   [3] W ii 21.25.

as an essayist or journalist. In common with other poor students of the time, he became tutor to the sons of prosperous local bourgeois; he made friends with the brothers Berens, rich merchants in the city of Riga,[1] whither they persuaded him to accompany them. Christoph Berens was an enlightened man with a great faith in the then rising science of economics, and directed Hamann's attention to the French economic writing of the time. Hamann translated a book by the French economist Dangeul, adding an appendix of his own, in the course of which, after an autobiographical excursus – in imitation of Young's *Night Thoughts* rather than Rousseau – about his sad career as an usher, his misanthropy, and the various attacks of gloom and melancholia which he had endured, he manages to quote Terence, Cicero, Madame de Graffigny, Gellert, Xenophon, Montesquieu, Plutarch, Pope, Hume, the early Councils of the Church, Plato, Mandeville, Aeneas Sylvius, the Marchese Belloni, Mathurin Régnier and the political testament of a head of a gang of smugglers. He praises the French Encyclopaedia and ends with a great paean to merchants as such, men engaged in increasing material welfare, in cultivating the arts of peace, as against the robber barons, the idle and corrupt monks of the Middle Ages, the hideous wars that devastated mankind, to which he favourably compares the eighteenth century as an age of peace.[2] If Plato and Aeneas Sylvius had lived now and had been acquainted with the Berenses they would not have looked down on trade and despised as they did the merchants of the Piraeus or the bankers of Italy. Trade is a form of altruistic benevolence, commerce brings blessings greater than Hobbes's or Machiavelli's bloodstained despots.

[1] In our day the capital of Latvia (then called Livonia).

[2] The Wars of the Spanish and Austrian Successions, the rumblings which culminated in the Seven Years War, and the Anglo-French wars, as well as the colonial wars in India and elsewhere, seem to have made no impact on him.

All this was conventional enough, and the Berenses must have been well pleased: they were progressive merchants and anxious to embellish their commercial activities with the works of polite culture. They liked to dabble in economics themselves, and although Hamann was obviously an odd fish, with an irregular imagination unlike that of the tidier imitators of the French style of which Germany could at that time boast a good number, he did honour to the house.

From time to time Hamann quarrelled with his patrons and became tutor in the houses of the German nobility along the Baltic coast. He was thin-skinned and resented the mixture of patronage and philistinism for which the Baltic barons were then (and indeed later) noted. His meditation on his mother's Christian death, with its epigraph from Young ('He mourns the Dead, who lives as they desire'),[1] is a totally conventional piece. In 1756 he could have been written down as a minor German imitator of French critics, with a special interest in economics,[2] a reader of Voltaire and Montesquieu and the abbé Coyer, a friend of liberty and equality, a defender of civic virtue and public spirit. In short, Hamann is at this stage a spokesman of the rising bourgeoisie, and against soldiers and nobles; one of those progressive youths who agreed with Kant and their common friend Berens that 'well earned' rightly fills the middle-class citizen with as much pride as 'well born' fills

---

[1] Edward Young, *Night Thoughts* (1742–5) ii 24, quoted at w ii 233.

[2] He retained this interest even after he changed his central opinions, as is shown by his appreciation of the writings of the Neapolitan abbé Galiani. It should be added, though, that Galiani's views were somewhat unorthodox: he argued against free trade and *laissez-faire*, laid stress on non-economic considerations of a social 'welfare state' type, and was not uncritical of Montesquieu. See Ferdinando Galiani, *Dialogues sur le commerce des bleds* (London, 1770), and Philip Merlan, 'Parva Hamanniana: Hamann and Galiani', *Journal of the History of Ideas* 11 (1950), 486–9.

an aristocrat.[1] All this was shared by Lessing, Diderot, Quesnay and all champions of progress and private enterprise, peace and enlightenment, and was common enough at the time.[2] If Hamann had died then he would have deserved his present obscurity; but in 1756 he undertook a journey that was destined to alter his life.

It is not quite clear why Hamann was sent to London in 1756. We know that the firm of the Berenses entrusted him with a mission that he failed to fulfil. The exact nature of this mission remains, to this day, a mystery. There may be some grounds for believing that it was political as well as commercial. His task, so some researchers suppose, was to deliver a proposal to leading circles in British political life that they should consider the possibility of the secession of the 'German' Baltic area from the Russian Empire to form an independent or semi-independent State, a scheme likely to appeal to England because of its assumed fear of the expanding Russian power. If this is so, it came to nothing, and if any record of it exists, it has not so far been found.

The year 1756, according to Swedenborg, was to precede the Last Judgement, in which the old Church was to be consumed and the new, 'true' universal Church of true Christianity was to rise like a phoenix from its ashes. Although the world in general experienced no noticeable cataclysm of this type, this is precisely what occurred within Hamann himself. The crisis in his life transformed him and created the figure that was, in its turn, to do much to alter the thought of his time.

[1] Berens's remark is quoted by Herder in *Briefe zu Beförderung der Humanität*: see *Herders Sämmtliche Werke*, ed. Bernhard Suphan, vol. 17 (Berlin, 1881), p. 391.

[2] See Philip Merlan, 'Parva Hamanniana: J. G. Hamann as a Spokesman of the Middle Class', *Journal of the History of Ideas* 9 (1948), 380–4, and Jean Blum, *La Vie et l'oeuvre de J.-G. Hamann, le 'Mage du Nord', 1730–1788* (Paris, 1912), pp. 32–3.

Of all the German provinces of the middle years of the eighteenth century, Prussia was the most consciously and vigorously progressive. Driven by the restless energy and ambition of Frederick the Great, the enlightened bureaucracy of Berlin was making a great and continuous effort to raise the social, economic and cultural level of Prussia to that of the admired lands of the West, in the first place of France, the supremacy of whose capital city was acknowledged by the entire civilised world. Industry and trade, with State aid and control, were created, encouraged, developed; finances were rationalised, agriculture improved; foreign savants, especially Frenchmen, were invited and made much of at the court in Potsdam. The language of the court was French. Frenchmen were not only appointed to leading intellectual positions – of these Voltaire, Maupertuis and La Mettrie were only the most famous – but put in charge of administrative departments, to the distress of all true Prussians (particularly in the traditional Eastern part of the country), who grumbled but obeyed. Every effort was made to rescue the country from the long-drawn effects of the collapse of much of German life and civilisation as a result of the murderous Thirty Years War, and the national humiliation and the enormous social and cultural night that followed. The policy of relatively enlightened paternalism which had begun with Frederick William, the Great Elector of Brandenburg, and the ferocious martinet, his grandson, Frederick William I of Prussia, was raised to a new height of ruthless efficiency by the great King. He was himself an accomplished writer and composer, besides being a soldier and administrator of genius, and the emergence of enlightened merchants like the Berenses in East Prussia and the Baltic, and the intellectual revival, of which Kant and the Academy in Berlin were among the leaders, were in complete harmony with this new awakening of the national energies.

This was the world in which, it was hoped, the young

Hamann would play his part. His friends knew that he was not a typical child of the Enlightenment, that his peculiar blend of religious and economic reading, his failure to distinguish himself in the Law, which he had officially studied at the University of Königsberg, the alternating indolence and spurts of sudden energy that drove him in unexpected directions, his lack of system, his spells of melancholia, his stammer, his morbid pride, which led him to quarrel with his patrons, his inability to settle down to any fixed occupation, did not make him an ideal official or littérateur in a centralised modern State consumed with desire for power and success, as well as a craving for the cultural development, influenced by Paris, of which such *Aufklärer* as Lessing, Mendelssohn, Nicolai were the leaders. Nevertheless, it was clear that men like Kant and his other Königsberg friends hoped that Hamann's natural abilities and imagination could somehow be disciplined and rendered useful. What they did not realise was that, despite his earlier, apparently conformist, adherence to the Enlightenment, he was by temperament violently opposed to the whole system: that he was basically a seventeenth-century man born into an alien world – religious, conservative, 'inner-directed', unable to breathe in the bright new world of reason, centralisation, scientific progress. Like Samuel Johnson in England, he represented an older attitude: personal relationships, inner life, meant more to him at all times than any of the values of the external world. He turned out to abhor the ideals of a typical 'progressive'; he hated the great Frederick, the 'Solomon of Prussia',[1] and his secular wisdom. Like the Russian Slavophils of the following century, he saw the family as the basis of true human existence, and the loose texture founded on affection, tradition, local – even provincial – values, with the minimum of interference by trained experts and remote officials, as the only tolerable

[1] e.g. w ii 320.29, w iii 55–60.

foundation of a truly Christian life. He was never an atheist or an agnostic. He seems never to have been tempted by the new, intellectually free, anti-clerical Franco-Prussian Establishment. He may not have known this before the journey to London, and his bold economic views and natural hatred of despotism may have deceived him, as it did his friends, concerning his prospects and vocation. But they were to learn with whom they were dealing soon enough.

After a leisurely journey through Berlin, where he made the acquaintance of Moses Mendelssohn, Nicolai and the other leading men of letters of that intellectual capital of the German world, followed by visits to Lübeck, Bremen, Hamburg, Amsterdam, Leiden and Rotterdam, he arrived in London on 18 April 1757. After an apparently abortive call at the Russian Embassy on his mysterious mission, he established himself in the house of a music teacher and decided to taste all the pleasures of the rich life of this great Western city. He tried to cure himself of stammering, attempted to learn to play the lute, and plunged into what he later described as a life of terrible dissipation. We have no independent evidence of what occurred, save his own account, which is that of a repentant sinner. At the end of ten months he was in debt to the extent of £300 and in a state of utter loneliness, misery and, at times, dreadful despair. He discovered accidentally that his host, the musician, was involved in a homosexual relationship with a 'rich Englishman',[1] and the appalling shock seems to have been the occasion of the great spiritual crisis of his life.

His mission was a failure; he was penniless, alone – above all alone – and no one understood what he was saying. He prayed for a friend to lead him out of the hideous labyrinth. He returned to his earlier life; he left the musician's house, established himself in a humble boarding-house and returned to his pietist beginnings: he did what pietists did

[1] W ii 37.7.

in states of spiritual oppression – he read the Bible from cover to cover. He had done so before, but now he found at last 'the Friend in my own heart, whither he had found his way when I felt nothing but void, darkness, desolation'.[1] He was starved of love and now he had found it. He began his real reading of the Bible on 13 March 1758 and, in pietist fashion, noted his spiritual progress day by day.[2] He wrote shortly afterwards, like a true disciple of Luther, that beneath the letter that is the flesh there is also an immortal soul, the breath of God, of light and life, a light burning in the darkness, which one must have eyes to see.[3]

Hamann emerged from this experience transformed. He had received no mystical vision, no specific revelation, as some converts to the new mystical trends then rising in Europe – partly in alliance with, partly in violent opposition to, the free individualist traditions of the Enlightenment – had often claimed to have had. There was no kind of connection between him and the Martinists or Freemasons or the many illuminist sects whose German centres were in East Prussia and Bavaria. He had been converted to the religion of his childhood, to Lutheran Protestantism. It is his application of this new light, which burned for him until the end of his days, that gives him historical importance.

[1] w ii 39.40.

[2] Rudolf Unger, in his excellent if somewhat ponderous *Hamanns Sprachtheorie im Zusammenhange seines Denkens: Grundlegung zu einer Würdigung der geistesgeschichtlichen Stellung des Magus in Norden* (Munich, 1905) – incorporated, in expanded form, into his *Hamann und die Aufklärung* (Jena, 1911) – points to parallels in the instructions on the reading of the Scriptures by such pietists as Francke in 1693 and Joachim Lange in 1733. This is highly plausible, although Hamann never became an orthodox pietist and broke out in all kinds of – from the orthodox point of view of the movement – worrying and unaccountable directions. His relation to pietism is somewhat analogous to, say, Blake's relation to the Nonconformist and Swedenborgian currents in which he was brought up.

[3] w i 315.7.

To what was he converted? Not just to the simple faith
of his childhood, but to the doctrine known to all those
who are familiar with the writings of the German Protestant
mystics and their followers in Scandinavia and England,
according to whom the sacred history of the Jews is not
merely an account of how that nation was guided from
darkness to light by God's almighty hand, but is a timeless
allegory of the inner history of the soul of each individual
man. The sins of individuals are like the sins of nations.
Hamann's own religious conversion in London took the form
of discovering in himself all the crimes of the children of
Israel: just as they stumbled and fell and worshipped idols,
so he fell into hedonism and materialism and intellectualism
and fell away from God; and as the balm of divine grace
enabled them to rise and return to the Lord and repent their
sins and resume their painful pilgrimage, so he too returned
to his Father and the Christ within him, was born again,
wept with bitter contrition and was saved. The story of the
wanderings of the Israelites, their *Reisekarte*, he declared,
was the story of his life, his *Lebenslauf*. This was the inner
sense of the biblical words. He who understood them understood himself – all understanding of anything whatever was
self-understanding, for the spirit alone is what can be understood, and to find it man need only, and must only, look
within himself. God's word was the ladder between heaven
and earth sent to aid weak and foolish children – it alone
would vouchsafe them a glimpse of what they were and why
they were as they were, and what their place was, and what
they must do and what avoid. The Bible was a great universal allegory, a similitude of that which was occurring everywhere and at every instant. So indeed were human history,
and nature properly understood – understood with the eyes
not of analytical reason but of faith, trust in God, self-
examination, for all these were one.

The rest of his life story is comparatively irrelevant. He
returned to the house of his patron, Berens, who treated

him with great sympathy and immediately began to con-
spire with Kant to obtain a new post for him. Kant suggested that they might write a primer on physics together,
but their difference of approach made collaboration impossible.[1] Hamann proposed marriage to Berens's sister
Katharina, but withdrew his offer, because her brother
vetoed it. He made one or two journeys to his friends on
the Baltic coast and then took an ill-paid post in the office
of the Department of War and Crown Lands. This he kept
for a while, but it brought in too little even for his modest
requirements – he was fond of food and drink but otherwise
his pleasures were few. He returned to his father's house
and collaborated in the *Königsbergsche Gelehrte und Politische
Zeitungen*, an enterprise financed by the bookseller Kanter,
who had always been exceptionally kind to him, lent him
books and encouraged him in every way. He began pub-
lishing his strange but arresting pamphlets: fragments,
unfinished essays, peculiar amalgams of philosophy, literary
criticism, philology, history and personal testimony, and
attracted the attention of the Berlin literati, who tried to
lure this strange talent into their circle – unsuccessfully, as
they soon realised. He did not marry but lived with one of
his father's servants, to whom he remained faithful all his
life and by whom he had four children. She was a simple,
illiterate and affectionate woman, and he was happy to use
this as an excuse for declining posts that might embarrass

[1] Nobody, Hamann says, can speak to children who cannot descend
to their level, that is, who does not love them. How can a crafty, vain
intellectual do this? (There may be something of Rousseau in this, the
defence of the value of emotional *rapport*, but Rousseau dealt in vast
ideas, whereas Hamann insists on concrete cases intuitively selected.)
No philosopher will sacrifice enough *amour propre* to predigest food for
children. Yet this is what God did for man – he abased himself, told
him stories, descended to his level, became man, suffered. This is what
the schoolmaster must do. Physics is too abstract. History or Natural
History is better. Genesis is best of all. All this he embodied in a letter
to Kant (B i 446–7), who did not reply.

her. From journalism he returned again to public service and in 1767 became an official in the General Excise and Customs Administration, then managed by one of Frederick's French experts, with whom Hamann remained on the worst of terms. He had by this time met Herder, who became his faithful and passionate disciple and, as he himself grew more famous and influential, spread his master's word throughout German-speaking lands.

Hamann occupied himself with attacks on liberal theologians – to him more contemptible than atheists – in obscure polemical pamphlets to which he gave grotesque titles. The flirtation with Mendelssohn, too, soon came to an end and was succeeded by one with F. K. von Moser, an enlightened bureaucrat who was fascinated by his originality. He corresponded with the Swiss pastor Lavater, who was the greatest champion of the varieties of illuminism and religious experience of his age, and became celebrated for his theory according to which analysis of physiognomies provided the key to knowledge of the varieties of character, disposition and talent. He travelled occasionally to Western Germany, and at least once to Poland. In later years he met the philosopher F. H. Jacobi, one of the most famous thinkers of his day, and conquered his head and heart; Jacobi replaced Herder in his affections and became his most devoted and admiring pupil. Towards the end of his life he gave up his post, which appeared to him beset by unspeakable humiliations and acts of meanness directed by his superiors against himself personally. He cannot have been a very competent official: all his life he remained obsessed by the thought that his hatred of abstraction was itself a sufficient guarantee of his practical nature and capacities. His last years were spent in comfort, for the affluent Jacobi introduced him to an even richer religious seeker named Buchholtz and to an *exaltée* lady, the Princess Golitsyn – the German widow of a Russian diplomat. Although Buchholtz seems to have been a little odd, Princess Golitsyn was perfectly sane – a Catholic who looked upon Hamann as a saint at whose hands she obtained the greatest spiritual comfort of her life. He died in her house in Münster in 1788, and is buried nearby – a peculiar and enigmatic figure to the end.

Hamann was not unaware of some of his defects, and was frequently self-deprecating. He declared: 'I feel at home in no occupation, I am no use either as a thinker or as a businessman . . . I cannot bear either high society or cloistered solitude';[1] 'I cannot think badly enough of myself';[2] 'I have always been stupid';[3] 'imbecility is the proper word for me';[4] he was, like Socrates, an 'ignoramus';[5] his mind was 'blotting paper' and retained only confused general impressions.[6] He constantly testifies that his own appalling style inspired in him nothing but disgust and horror, that he did not expect to be read much – for ninety-nine readers out of a hundred his work is a hopeless business.[7] He wished that he had remained a merchant. He knew that the sign of genius is the elimination of the superfluous, the expression of the most powerful thought in the smallest number of words, and that he was far from attaining his goal. Yet in spite of all this he half accepted the recognition of his genius by Herder, Jacobi and his other disciples.

He had a certain desire to remain mysterious, a riddle to his contemporaries. When Kant begged him to talk in human language and even the loyal Herder confessed to being unable to make his way through some of the dark words showered upon him, he defended himself by saying that not everyone can be a system-building spider,[8] and that passion for system

---

[1] B vii 193.25.   [2] B vi 128.34.   [3] B vi 270.17.
[4] B v 365.17.   [5] B iv 4.16.
[6] B iv 7.4; cf. B vii 27.35.   [7] B ii 85.20.
[8] B ii.203.37. The pun on *Spinne* (the German for 'spider') and Spinoza probably proved irresistible to Hamann; his work may well be fuller of puns than that of any other thinker.

is a form of vanity.[1] True, he does not attain to precision and systematic exposition, he is only 'fit for fragments, leaps, hints',[2] but then system is an obstacle to the discovery of the truth.[3] This is a reference to Kant. '[M]a seule règle c'est de n'en point avoir.'[4] 'I look on the best demonstration in philosophy', he wrote to Kant, 'as the sensible girl looks on a love letter'[5] – with pleasure but suspicion.

He did not underestimate himself: he claimed to be original, to walk by himself, to put imitators to flight. He saw himself as a precursor, as an antinomian, a Socratic gadfly; he complacently accepted Herder's portrait of him as a Columbus who had discovered wholly new territories, and in a letter to Mendelssohn congratulating him on his marriage he said '*genius* is a crown of thorns, *taste* is a purple cloak to cover a back torn by whips'.[6] And indeed his style is appalling: twisted, dark, allusive, filled with digressions, untraceable references, private jokes, puns within puns and invented words, cryptograms, secret names for persons in the past or present, for ideas, for the inexpressible contents of visions of the truth; where the spirit cannot be conveyed by the verbal flesh he attempts at once to imitate and emulate the cabbalistic utterances, justly forgotten, of mystagogues of the past, in phrases where it is impossible to tell where imitation ceases and parody begins. He remained unread, save for such discoverers as Kierkegaard, who revered him, and gives the impression that he thought him one of the only true philosophers of his time, speaking of his 'enormous genius'.[7]

[1] B i 367.13.   [2] B i 431.30.   [3] B vi 350.6.

[4] *Mittheilungen aus dem Tagebuch und Briefwechsel der Fürstin Adelheid Amalia von Gallitzin nebst Fragmenten und einem Anhange* (Stuttgart, 1868), p. 24.

[5] B i 378.32.   [6] B ii 168.23.

[7] Howard V. Hong and Edna H. Hong (eds), *Søren Kierkegaard's Journals and Papers* [hereunder *Journals*], vol. 2, F–K (Bloomington/London, 1970), p. 252. [Kierkegaard's admiration for Hamann, though undoubtedly deep, was not unbounded, as he himself makes explicit

The fault is, quite deliberately, his own. 'What for others is style, for me is soul.'[1] Mendelssohn tells no more than the truth when he says that Hamann's style is too *outré*, too twisted, exaggerated, impenetrable, there are too many hobby-horses, family jokes intelligible only to esoteric cliques – 'what a mishmash of satirical fancies, wild spiritual

---

in *Concluding Unscientific Postscript*: pp. 223–4 in the translation by David F. Swenson (London, 1941). Walter Lowrie's opinion, which has influenced other critics, is that Hamann 'is the only author by whom S. K. was profoundly influenced': *Kierkegaard* (London etc., 1938), p. 164. This seems to be an exaggeration: indeed, in *Johann Georg Hamann: An Existentialist* (Princeton, 1950), p. 4, Lowrie observes disarmingly that this view 'has perhaps more truth than evidence on its side'. Certainly he misused one piece of evidence, by sponsoring the odd myth that Kierkegaard called Hamann 'Emperor'. In *Kierkegaard*, Lowrie writes (pp. 164–5) that 'he hailed him reverently as "Emperor!" the very first time he made mention of him in the Journal'; he then refers to the journal entry for 10 September 1836. But apart from the fact that Kierkegaard refers to Hamann the day before (*Journals*, vol. 2, p. 158), in terms that suggest previous acquaintance with his work, Lowrie's reading of the entry for 10 September is bizarre. Here is the whole entry, translated by the Hongs: 'In an age when it is the order of the day for one author to plunder another, it is nevertheless pleasant at times to stumble upon men whose individuality so moulds and stamps every word with their portrait that it must compel everyone who meets it in a strange place to say to those concerned: "Render unto Caesar what is Caesar's"' (*Journals*, vol. 1, A–E (1967), p. 53). In the first place, why is this passage thought to be about Hamann specifically? Kierkegaard does refer to Hamann in a postscript added the same day to an earlier passage (*Journals*, vol. 2, p. 199), but neither this nor his reference to Hamann on the previous day (in an entry principally about Goethe) seems conclusive. In the second place, whoever is referred to is plainly not being called 'Emperor' (though the Danish for 'Caesar' – 'Keiser' – can certainly be translated 'Emperor' in suitable contexts). Lowrie seems to have misread Kierkegaard's straightforward use of Jesus' well-known remark. (Another claim, that Kierkegaard called Hamann his 'only master', is perhaps equally without foundation. See Walter Leibrecht, *God and Man in the Thought of Hamann* (Philadelphia, 1966), p. 5, where no reference is given. I have been unable to find this phrase in Kierkegaard's works.) Ed.]

[1] B iii 378.36; cf. B iii 104.26.

leaps, flowery allusions, outlandish metaphors, critical vaticinations! – interlarded with passages from the Bible, decorated with Latin and English verse and frequent references to Plato, Bacon, Michaelis, Ausonius, Wachter, Holy Writ, Petronius, Shakespeare, Roscommon, Young, Voltaire and a hundred others'[1] – and gives up the case as desperate. Yet Mendelssohn felt that there was something remarkable about Hamann, that he was quite unlike any other writer who had lived. He realised that he had to do with a hostile genius who looked with contempt and indignation upon the doctrines of himself and his friends. And indeed Hamann's attitude towards the enlightened rationalists of Berlin was not unlike Rousseau's towards the *philosophes* and Encyclopaedists in Paris, only more so; still more like that of D. H. Lawrence towards Keynes, Russell, Moore and the whole of Bloomsbury, whose very existence appeared to him an insult to the forces of life and nature that he worshipped. Like Rousseau and Lawrence, Hamann was prepared to like individual members of this worthless group; he liked Kant personally and criticised him without bothering to understand his doctrines, much as Lawrence attacked English intellectuals; he accepted help from Kant without returning hatred for it, and called him a nice little homunculus, agreeable to gossip with, though plainly blind to the truth. He was flattered by the attentions of Mendelssohn and his friends, though in the end he turned against them, personally as well as ideologically; and he retained some admiration for Lessing, despite his deplorable Spinozism and calm rationalism, which seemed to Hamann to rob the world and the human spirit of all passion and colour. Lessing was not interested in him; but Mendelssohn, the most just and unprejudiced of the Prussian intellectuals, detected something unique and original and important. And he was not mistaken.

---

[1] *Moses Mendelssohn's gesammelte Schriften*, ed. G. B. Mendelssohn, vol. 4, part 2 (Leipzig, 1844), p. 410.

3 THE CENTRAL CORE

WHAT IS it that is today worth resuscitating in Hamann's views and personality? Hardly his theosophy, central though this was to himself, and interesting and important in the history of Protestant religious belief. He was neither the first nor the greatest of those who believed that the only path to understanding was revelation; that prayer, meditation, the Christian life and innocence of spirit made it easier for the soul to be made whole; that nature in its entirety could be viewed as a book in which, in great and luminous letters, the whole history of the world and of man could be read by those who knew how to read; that all things and events were a great hieroglyphic script that needed only a key, which God's words alone provided, to reveal the nature and the fate of man and his relationship to the world and to God. This is in various forms already to be found in Eckhart and Tauler and Böhme and the whole German mystical tradition, of which pietism was an inward-looking Lutheran branch.

Even though this was the heart of Hamann's new transfigured outlook, what was truly – and deeply – original was his conception of the nature of man, the method by which he established it, and the polemical use that he made of it. He hated his century with an almost pathological hatred, and attacked what was most characteristic in it with an unparalleled sharpness and strength. He was the first writer in modern days to denounce the Enlightenment and all its works, and not merely this or that error or crime of the new culture, as for instance Rousseau, even at his most violent, does – for Rousseau shares more presuppositions with the Encyclopaedists than he denies, and in any case conceals his inconsistencies beneath a torrent of marvellous rhetoric. Hamann rose in revolt against the entire structure of science, reason, analysis – its virtues even more than its vices. He thought the basis of it altogether false and its conclusions a blasphemy against the nature of man and his creator; and he looked for evidence not so much in theological or metaphysical axioms or dogmas or a priori arguments, which the Enlightenment, with some justification, thought that it had discredited as methods of argument, as in his own day-to-day experience, in the empirically – not intuitively – perceived facts themselves, in direct observation of men and their conduct, and in direct introspection of his own passions, feelings, thoughts, way of life.

These were weapons which, in the end, the Enlightenment could not afford to disregard. Romanticism, anti-rationalism, suspicion of all theories and intellectual constructions as at best useful fictions, at worst a distorting medium – a form of escape from facing reality itself – virtually begin with Hamann. There is more than something of this among the Neoplatonists of the Renaissance, in Pascal, and still more in Vico. But the frontal attack was delivered by him. The fact that it was often ill-conceived, overdone, naïve, ludicrously exaggerated and irresponsible, or touched with bitter and savage obscurantism and a blind hatred of some of the noblest moral and artistic – as well as intellectual – achievements of mankind, does not lessen its importance, even if it diminishes its value. For some of what is most original in Hamann turned out to be in large measure disturbingly valid. His enemies are both those he calls the Pharisees – the supporters of the great dogmatic establishments, the Church of Rome or the French monarchy and its servants and imitators in German lands – and those he speaks of as the Sadducees – the freethinkers in Paris or Berlin or Edinburgh. And even though their achievements are, and remain, very great, while Hamann's unbridled and indiscriminate onslaughts on them are often patently unjust and, at times, absurd, humanity has had to pay a heavy price for disregarding that which he was able to see – to pay in terms not only of intellectual error, but of the defective practice and appalling human suffering to which the influence of the doctrines of both these mutually antagonistic establishments has helped to lead. This alone makes Hamann's single-minded but tortuous ideas worth examining in a spirit necessarily very different from his own.

There is no true development in Hamann's thought after his conversion, neither development nor orderly exposition. His views – on the nature of man; on his modes of cognition (belief, knowledge, understanding, imagination, reasoning, faith); on nature, history, God; on language, genius, expression, creation; on the senses, the passions, the relations of body, will, mind; on history and politics; on the ends of man and his salvation – remained from the age of thirty until his death at the age of fifty-eight virtually unaltered. It does not matter where in his writings one begins: nothing has a beginning or a middle or an end; everything is called forth by an occasion – the desire to instruct a friend, to refute some enemy or perverter of the truth, to intrigue or puzzle some old acquaintance or adversary. The thread of argument, such as it is, is constantly broken by other arguments or topics, digressions within digressions, sometimes within one vast paragraph, and the continuity of the thought emerges, after a long passage in underground channels, in some unexpected place, and is once again soon buried under the luxuriant, irrepressible, chaotic, scattered tropical growth of Hamann's ideas and images, which at once exhilarated and maddened even his most devoted and worshipping friends.

Yet within this wild and tangled wood, beside which even the works of such unsystematic writers as Diderot or

Herder seem models of pedantic neatness, there is a unity of thought and outlook which no one who is not immediately repelled by his style and unparallelled obscurity will fail to grasp early in his reading. Neither his positive nor his negative doctrines are ever in serious doubt. The details may be puzzling or even exasperating; the main lines – for there are such – are firm and unchanged for over a quarter of a century of discontinuous but prolific writing. Goethe, who obtained from him, as from everyone else, precisely what he himself required, saw his thought as a kind of inner gesturing – the expression of his life by means of a kind of inward miming of it, which could be grasped only by feeling ourselves into his inner states, by a vision of the similes and allegories by which he sought to convey them.[1] Hamann's life, his style, his faith and his thought were one. His positive doctrines always developed as part of a furious onslaught on some falsehood to be rooted out: no man believed in or practised intellectual toleration less. So, for example, his doctrine of knowledge is rooted in a denunciation of Descartes' mathematical approach to natural science, and of the coherent structure of theoretical knowledge of man and nature embodied in the *Encyclopédie*, a work conceived and hatched in the hateful city of Paris – the work in which Kant, in one of his less tactful moments, suggested that Hamann, after he had returned from London out of a job and in debt, might find something to translate, for the benefit of his benighted fellow Prussians.

---

[1] Goethe's marvellous power of insight did not fail him: his remark that the Neapolitans had their own Hamann in 'grandfather' Giambattista Vico (in whom he took little interest) is a brilliant observation. See *Die Italienische Reise*, 5 March 1787: p. 28 in *Goethes Werke*, vol. 31 (Weimar, 1904).

4   THE ENLIGHTENMENT

IT IS worth remembering that Hamann's attitude to the *philosophes* and all their works was undoubtedly connected with the fact that his formative years were dominated, like those of many German thinkers of this period, by the rise of the new doctrines of the Enlightenment, which, despite opposition offered by the Churches, both Catholic and Protestant, and occasional persecution by civil authority, both in France and in parts of Italy, swiftly rose to be the most powerful movement in European thought.

There were many divisions within the movement itself. Contrary to the traditional histories of the subject, not every French Encyclopaedist or German rationalist believed that men were by nature good, and ruined only by the follies or wickedness of priests or rulers, or by crippling institutions. Some, like Montesquieu and Helvétius, each in his own fashion, believed that men were born neither good nor bad, but were largely moulded by environment or education or chance, or all of these, into what they became. Others, like La Mettrie and at times Voltaire, believed that men were by nature cruel, aggressive and weak, and had to be restrained from developing these undesirable dispositions by deliberately imposed disciplines. Some among the new philosophers believed in the existence of an immortal soul, some did not; some were deists (or even theists); others were agnostics or militant atheists. Some believed that natural environment – climate, geography, physical and physiological characteristics of a scarcely alterable kind – exercised a causal influence that wholly determined human behaviour;

others believed in the almost unlimited power of education and legislation, as weapons that men held in their own hands. Some, like Voltaire and Condorcet, paid attention to historical development; others, like Helvétius and Holbach, did not. Some, like d'Alembert and Condorcet, based their hopes upon the progress and application to human affairs of mathematics and natural science; others, like Mably, Rousseau, Raynal, Morelly, were inclined towards primitivism and dreamt about the restoration of a simple, innocent, pure-hearted society of 'natural' men, free from the deleterious influence of the corrupt life of the great cities and the tyranny of organised religion. Some believed in enlightened despotism, others in democracy; some, like Condorcet, believed in human equality; others, like Holbach and Kant, condemned the populations of entire continents as inferior races. Some conceived of the axioms and methods of discovery and knowledge as revealed a priori to special intellectual faculties or intuitive insight, and believed in natural law and natural rights; others believed that all knowledge rested on the experience of the physical senses, rejected all a priori certainty, and were rigorous empiricists. Some were determinists or utilitarians or teleologists; others believed in moral sense, or free will or chance.

Yet despite these disagreements – and they were far more profound than a cursory survey of the Enlightenment would indicate – there were certain beliefs that were more or less common to the entire party of progress and civilisation, and this is what makes it proper to speak of it as a single movement. These were, in effect, the conviction that the world, or nature, was a single whole, subject to a single set of laws, in principle discoverable by the intelligence of man; that the laws which governed inanimate nature were in principle the same as those which governed plants, animals and sentient beings; that man was capable of improvement; that there existed certain objectively recognisable human goals which all men, rightly so described, sought after, namely happiness, knowledge, justice, liberty, and what was somewhat vaguely described but well understood as virtue; that these goals were common to all men as such, were not unattainable, nor incompatible, and that human misery, vice and folly were mainly due to ignorance either of what these goals consisted in or of the means of attaining them — ignorance due in turn to insufficient knowledge of the laws of nature. Moreover, and despite the doubts expressed by Montesquieu and his followers, it was by and large believed that human nature was fundamentally the same in all times and places; local and historical variations were unimportant compared with the permanent central core in terms of which human beings could be defined as a single species, as minerals or plants or animals could be. Consequently the discovery of general laws that govern human behaviour, their clear and logical integration into scientific systems — of psychology, sociology, economics, political science and the like (although they did not use these names) — and the determination of their proper place in the great corpus of knowledge that covered all discoverable facts, would, by replacing the chaotic amalgam of guesswork, tradition, superstition, prejudice, dogma, fantasy and 'interested error' that hitherto did service as human knowledge and human wisdom (and of which by far the chief protector and instigator was the Church), create a new, sane, rational, happy, just and self-perpetuating human society, which, having arrived at the peak of attainable perfection, would preserve itself against all hostile influences, save perhaps those of the forces of nature.

This is the noble, optimistic, rational doctrine and ideal of the great tradition of the Enlightenment from the Renaissance until the French Revolution, and indeed beyond it, until our own day. The three strongest pillars upon which it rested were faith in reason, that is, a logically connected structure of laws and generalisations susceptible of demonstration or verification; in the identity of human nature through time and the possibility of universal human goals; and finally in the possibility of attaining to the second by means of the first, of ensuring physical and spiritual harmony and progress by the power of the logically or empirically guided critical intellect, which was in principle capable of analysing everything into its ultimate constituents, of discovering their interrelations and the single system of laws which they obeyed, and thereby of answering all questions capable of being formulated by clear minds intent upon discovering the truth.

Naturally the enormous success and prestige of Newtonian physics, which seemed to have accomplished precisely this in the realm of inanimate nature, vastly added to the confidence of moral and social thinkers, who saw no reason why the application of the same methods in these spheres should not in time yield equally universal and unalterable knowledge. Despite hesitations and reservations of an obvious kind, there was an ever-growing movement, especially in the Protestant Churches – but to some extent in that of Rome also – in favour of attempting to apply these methods in metaphysical and theological matters too: or, at any rate, showing that Christian beliefs were not incompatible with, but in many cases identical with, or complementary to, the new rationalism. The disciples of Leibniz and Wolff in Germany, as well as the schools of natural theology in England and Scotland, moved along these lines. Rational religion, rational metaphysics, rational politics, rational law – these doctrines appeared to be moving forward with the irresistible power of liberated human reason. The spirit that inspired the most fearless and humane and enlightened writing on the need for reform in the often hideously oppressive and irrational legal systems or economic policies, or for the elimination of political and moral injustices and absurdities which are today by and large forgotten, was the same as that which inspired progress in the physical and biological sciences; it occasionally led to such oddities as

29

Wolff's belief, enunciated in the course of an argument against miracles, that Christ was able to change water into wine, and Joshua to stop the sun at Gibeon, because they were endowed with superior – superhuman, indeed – chemical or astrophysical knowledge. All principles of explanation everywhere must be the same. Indeed, this is what rationality consisted in.

Not many thinkers of this period who are remembered today openly dissented from this central principle. Hamann was one of these. He attacked the entire outlook in every particular; and feeling himself a David chosen by the Lord to smite this vast and horrible Goliath, he marched to battle alone and unattended. He tried to attack the enemy along their entire front; and embodied his literally reactionary programme in three principal doctrines (if collections of beginnings without ends, ends without beginnings, riddles and epigrams and dark, though at times marvellously pregnant, sentences may be called that). These were: his view of the nature, the sources and the effectiveness of knowledge and belief; his theory of language and of symbolism generally; and his conception of genius, imagination, creation and the relation of God to man.

5   KNOWLEDGE

Historical, contingent truths can never be proofs of rational, necessary truths.

Lessing, 'Über den Beweis des Geistes und der Kraft' [1]

DESCARTES BELIEVED that it was possible to acquire knowledge of reality from a priori sources, by deductive reasoning. This, according to Hamann, is the first appalling fallacy of modern thought. The only true subverter of this false doctrine was Hume,[2] whom Hamann read with enthusiastic agreement. Indeed, it is not too much to say that the Bible and Hume are the two oddly interwoven roots of his ideas.

Hume had declared that the foundation of our knowledge of ourselves and the external world was *belief* – something for which there could be no a priori reasons; something to which all principles, theories, the most coherent and elaborate constructions of our minds, practical or theoretical, could in the end be reduced. We believed that there were

[1] Gotthold Ephraim Lessing, *Gesammelte Werke*, ed. Paul Rilla, vol. 8 (Berlin, 1956), p. 12.

[2] Locke, of course, had declared that the only source of true knowledge is, not rational intuition or self-evident timeless truths which critical reason cannot reject or doubt, but experience, the brute fact of sensation – the fact that we see what we see, hear what we hear, form the images that we do. But Locke equivocated, allowing a considerable role to analytic reason.

material objects round us that behaved in this or that way; we believed that we were identical with ourselves through time. In Hamann's words: 'Our own existence and the existence of all things outside us must be believed and cannot be determined in any other way.'[1] And again: 'Belief is not the product of the intellect, and can therefore also suffer no casualty by it: since *belief* has as little grounds as *taste* or *sight*.'[2] Belief gives us all our values, heaven and earth, morals and the real world. 'Know ye, philosophers, that between cause and effect, means and ends, the connection is not physical but spiritual, ideal; that is the nexus of blind faith.'[3] We do not perceive causes or necessity in nature; we believe them, we act as if they existed; we think and formulate our ideas in terms of such beliefs, but they are themselves mental *habits*, *de facto* forms of human behaviour, and the attempt to deduce the structure of the universe from them is a monstrous attempt to convert our subjective habits – which differ in different times and places and between different individuals – into unalterable, objective 'necessities' of nature.

Hamann read Hume with great attention. Hume was of course an unbeliever, an enemy of the Christian faith, but God spoke the truth through him all the same. He is a 'Saul among the Prophets',[4] a kind of Balaam, a reluctant witness to the truth, an ally despite himself.[5] Hamann translated Hume's *Dialogues concerning Natural Religion*, of which he thought most highly, and regarded Kant as a kind of Prussian Hume,[6] even though Kant ignored Hume's teaching on belief: where Hume is content to report that we can neither know nor reasonably ask why things are as they are, and must content ourselves with describing what

[1] W ii 73.21; cf. B vii 167.10.   [2] W ii 74.2.
[3] W iii 29.10.   [4] B i 380.6.
[5] See Philip Merlan, 'From Hume to Hamann', *Personalist* 32 (1951), 11–18.
[6] B iv 293.36.

we cannot help believing any more than we can help seeing, smelling, hearing, Kant attempts to erect these empirical habits into categories. 'Hume is always my man.'[1] The *Dialogues concerning Natural Religion* are 'full of poetic beauties' and 'not dangerous at all'.[2] 'To eat an egg, to drink a glass of water Hume needs belief;[3] . . . but if belief is needed even for eating or drinking, why does Hume break his own principle when judging of things higher than eating or drinking?'[4] All wisdom begins in sense. '*Wisdom* is *feeling*, the *feeling* of a *father* and a *child*';[5] and again, 'The existence of the smallest things rests on *immediate impression*, and not on *ratiocination*.'[6] Faith is the basis of our knowledge of the external world. We may crave for something else: logical deduction, guarantees given by infallible intuition. But Hume is right, all we have is a kind of animal faith. This is the great battering-ram with which Hamann seeks to destroy the edifice of traditional metaphysics and theology.

Hume's principle was that from one fact no other fact can be deduced, that necessity is a logical relation, that is, a relation between symbols and not between the real things in the world, and that all proponents of doctrines that claim to know existential propositions that are not based on experience, or to infer other existential propositions by methods of pure thought, are deceiving either themselves or others or both. To this Hamann held steadily all his life: it is the basis of his entire attack on the methods and values of the scientific Enlightenment. There are no innate ideas in the sense in which the rationalists, Descartes, Leibniz and the Platonists spoke of them. We depend on metabolism with external nature: 'The *senses* are to the *intellect* what the *stomach* is to the vessels which separate off the finer

---

[1] B iv 294.7.   [2] B iv 205.33, 34.
[3] Hamann delights in Hume's doctrine that even the most trivial act presupposes undemonstrable belief in certain uniformities.
[4] In his letter to Kant of 27 July 1759 (B i 379.35).
[5] B iii 35.1.   [6] B vii 460.6.

and higher *juices* of the blood: the blood-vessels abstract what they need from the stomach . . . our bodies are nothing but what comes from our or our parents' stomachs. The *stamina* and *menstrua* of our *reason* are properly only *revelation* and *tradition*.'[1] Tradition is accumulation of past beliefs; revelation is God's appearance to us through nature, or through Holy Writ.

Apart from the metaphysical implications of this, Hamann's constantly repeated point is that revelation is direct contact between one spirit and another, God and ourselves. What we see, hear, understand, is directly given. Yet we are not mere passive receptacles, as Locke had taught: our active and creative powers are empirical attributes that different men or societies have in different degrees and kinds, so that no generalisations can be guaranteed to hold for too long. Hamann boldly turns Hume's scepticism into an affirmation of belief – in empirical knowledge – that is its own guarantee: the ultimate datum, for which it makes no sense to ask for some general rationale.

In this way Hamann turns those very empirical weapons that were earlier used against dogmatic theology and metaphysics against rationalist epistemology – Cartesian, Leibnizian, Kantian – as his admirer Kierkegaard used them against the Hegelians. Nature and observation become weapons against a priori or quasi-a-priori guarantees of progress, or axioms for natural sciences, or any other large, metaphysically grounded, world-enveloping schemas. The metaphysician Fichte was right from this point of view to exclaim that empiricism was or could be a danger to Rousseau and the French Revolution and the absolute principles which they had invoked. Hamann is among the earliest empiricist reactionaries who seek to blow up the constructions of audacious scientific reason by appeals – somewhat like Burke's, but much further-reaching and more radical –

[1] w iii 39.7.

to asymmetrical, untidy reality, the reality revealed to a vision not distorted by metaphysical spectacles, or by knowledge of the certain existence of the cut and dried pattern which one professes to be attempting to find; for there is no knowledge without belief, unreasoned belief, at its base.

All general propositions rest on this. All abstractions are, in the end, arbitrary. Men cut reality, or the world of their experience, as they wish, or as they are used to doing, without any special warrant from nature, which has no grooves of an a priori kind. Yet our most famous philosophers cut away the branch on which they are sitting, hide with shame, like Adam, their unavoidable and agreeable sin;[1] they deny the brute fact, the irrational. Things are as they are; without accepting this there is no knowledge, for all knowledge reposes on belief or faith, *Glaube* (that is the transition that Hamann makes without argument), faith in the existence whether of chairs and tables and trees, or of God and the truth of his Bible, all given to faith, to belief, to no other faculty. The contrast between faith and reason is for him a profound fallacy. There are no ages of faith followed by ages of reason. These are fictions. Reason is built on faith, it cannot replace it; there are no ages that are not ages of both: the contrast is unreal. A rational religion is a contradiction in terms. A religion is true not because it is rational but because it is face to face with what is real: modern philosophers pursue rationality like Don Quixote, and will in the end, like him, lose their wits. Existence logically precedes reason; that is to say, what exists cannot be demonstrated by reason but must first be experienced itself, and then one may, if one wishes, build rational structures upon it whose reliability can be no greater than the reliability of the original base. There exists a pre-rational reality;[2] how we arrange it is ultimately arbitrary.

[1] w iii 190.23.   [2] w iii 191.24.

This is in effect modern existentialism in embryo – its growth can be traced from Böhme and the German mystics to Hamann and from him to Jacobi and Kierkegaard and Nietzsche and Husserl; the route taken by Merleau-Ponty and Sartre springs from it too, but its twists and turns are another story. In this chain Hamann's views are an irremovable link.

Among eighteenth-century German thinkers both the rationalist Lessing and the irrationalist Jacobi were profoundly troubled by the 'abyss' between the general statements of philosophy and empirical reality, between the universal 'truths of reason' and the 'truths of fact' that Leibniz had distinguished. Lessing agonised over the question of how necessary truths, *quod semper, quod ubique, quod ab omnibus*, say the existence of God, or of the immortal soul, or universal objective moral truths – the 'truths of reason' – could be inferred from historical propositions, empirically known, and therefore contingent. God spoke to men at identifiable times, in particular places, Jesus was crucified in a particular place at a particular time, certain Apostles stated holy truths, had had experiences, commonly called supernatural, in specific places at specific times: can the eternal truths revealed by this *historia sacra* rest on accounts which no evidence could render absolute, infallible? How can this be accepted? He concluded by wondering whether, with the progress of human knowledge, knowledge of these contingent and empirical propositions would gradually lead to necessary truths, knowable a priori, guaranteed for ever; and concluded in turn from this that in the meanwhile all approaches towards them of all the various religions were but tentative efforts to arrive at the single central truth – hence that all these various avenues had an equal right to our respect and veneration; and deduced from this principles of universal tolerance embodied in the celebrated tale of the three rings in his play *Nathan the Wise*. Yet how could 'historical, contingent truths . . . be proofs of rational, necessary truths'?[1] They cannot. 'This is the loathsome wide ditch', Lessing wrote, 'across which I cannot get, however often and earnestly I have attempted to leap over it',[2] and pathetically cries for light. Yet surely necessary truths exist? What then is their rational foundation? Jacobi maintained that Lessing died an atheist; Moses Mendelssohn hotly denied this – Lessing, he claimed, died a believer. Whatever the truth, the problem remained.

Jacobi in his turn was tormented by what he called the gap between his heart and his head: 'The light is in my heart,' he said: 'but as soon as I seek to carry it to my intellect it goes out.'[3] On one side the chilly system of science, on the other hand the real world, which he is given only by the ardent fire of inner conviction – Jacobi cannot find the path between the direct experience of the heart and the general propositions of reason or science, which appear not to have any point of contact. He opts for the heart: the truths of faith. But does not the problem remain? Hamann attacks Lessing and tries to help Jacobi: but for him there is no real problem, no 'loathsome ditch', no abyss. What can it mean to wish to 'explain' existence? Thought – or rather thoughts, ideas, indeed all psychological events – are part of the furniture of the universe. There is no point outside the universe at which one can place oneself, from which the universe can be judged, condemned, justified, explained, proved. There is no chasm here: an infinity of reasons cannot be integrated into one trivial fact. In a letter to Jacobi Hamann wrote:

> Metaphysics has its own school and court languages . . . and I am incapable of either understanding or making use of them. Hence I am close to suspecting that the whole of our philosophy consists more of language than of reason, and the misunderstandings of countless words, the personification of

---

[1] loc. cit. (p. 31 above, note 1).   [2] ibid., p. 14.
[3] *Friedrich Heinrich Jacobi's Werke*, vol. 1 (Leipzig, 1812), p. 367.

arbitrary abstractions . . . have generated an entire world of problems which it is as vain to try to solve as it was to invent them.[1]

These problems are false problems. The whole world of the a priori is a fiction. Hamann is as certain of this as Bishop Berkeley was, or any modern positivist. One must avoid imposing one's own theoretical fancies upon the world. The tendency of reason is to invent entities, to start from what is given in sense and then inflate this into 'ideas of pure reason' or notions of 'pure being'. Nobody has ever understood what Aristotle or Kant really mean. Wisdom is one of the fruits of the tree of life. All evil comes from the tree of science. One should say 'est ergo sum', otherwise one will construct some brilliant fiction which one will worship as an idol. Jacobi thinks that there is some special faculty, a Pascalian 'reason of the heart', some irrational power, some special sense, whereby he will attain to ultimate reality and God; he oscillates between Spinoza and Plato, and chooses Plato. Hamann complains that what Jacobi is asking for is some special organ, a special set of contingent truths which will be more than contingent, and this is absurd. To know what there is we must look, feel, construct hypotheses perhaps, but suspect them as constructions of our own, above all not allow them to usurp the place of direct experience. The fact that experience differs from age to age, or even individual to individual, is nothing against it. Universalism is an idle craving, an attempt to reduce the rich variety of the universe to a bleak uniformity, which is itself a form of not facing reality, attempting to imprison it in some prefabricated favourite logical envelope – an insult to creation and a piece of foolish and unpardonable presumption on the part of those who try to do so. All forms of religious apologetics are this too, an

[1] B V 272.3.

attempt to apologise for, explain away, direct experience of God – whether in mystical revelation or by reading and understanding his word or deciphering his writing in nature – in terms invented by the puny intellect of the individual; an attempt to domesticate God, to place him in some tame herbarium of one's own.

In psychological terms it could be said that in Hamann the insulted faith of the defeated, humiliated Germans flared up against the Western oppressor with his levelling rationalism, and blasted a path for a general protest and campaign against the entire scientific-philosophical establishment, and in due course in every other province – in history, in literature, in politics, wherever the rational spirit made its home. Hamann sometimes says that he obtained these ideas from Young's *Night Thoughts*. If so, Young can hardly have known what a Pandora's box he was opening. Young preached the need for letting nature grow organically in the dark soil of faith and the past. But this turned into something much more formidable, into a general attack upon rationalism in all spheres, much as some of the most characteristic doctrines of our own century – existentialism in philosophy or Barthian anti-rationalism in religion, the doctrines of Heidegger and his pupils, emotivism in ethics, surrealism in art, and all the other manifestations of rebellion against the positivism of the late nineteenth century and the early twentieth – are symptoms of a profound malaise. In this sense Saint-Simon and Maistre, from their very different points of view, correctly identified Luther as the earliest and greatest rebel against the established order – the incarnation of that force that destroyed order in France in 1789 and, despite all the Protestant quietism and advocacy of resignation, opened the door to the individual desire for self-assertion that had been outraged by the uniformity imposed upon it.

Direct experience for Hamann is a concrete fact – the basis of all true knowledge of reality. Its enemy is system, which of necessity is composed of words denoting abstractions or numbers. 'With numbers, as with words, one can do anything one likes.'[1] All these are *entia rationis*, which philosophers have taught us to confound with real things. How do such philosophers operate? By 'tearing up what nature has joined and uniting what it has divided'.[2] Analysis dismembers (although it cannot destroy), synthesis combines (although it cannot literally fuse).[3] 'Only a *scholastic intelligence* divides itself into realism and idealism; a correct and genuine intellect knows nothing of such imaginary divisions.'[4] Analysis and synthesis are equally arbitrary.[5] The fault of all philosophers is to introduce arbitrary divisions, to shut their eyes to reality in order to build 'castles in the air'.[6] The language of nature is not mathematics – God is a poet, not a geometer.[7] Conventional signs are needed, no doubt, but they are unreal. Words like 'cause', 'reason', 'universality' are mere counters, and do not correspond to things. The greatest error in the world is 'to confuse *words* with *concepts* and *concepts* with *real things*'.[8] Philosophers are imprisoned in their own systems, which have become as dogmatic as those of the Church. Hamann said apropos of Kant: 'Every systematiser must be expected to look on his system precisely as every Catholic looks on his true Church.'[9] The geometrical method may do for spiders like Spinoza who catch flies in their nets,[10] but to apply it to living experience, to regard words like 'reason', 'existence' as referring to anything other than relationships that do not

---

[1] B vii 441.22; cf. w iii 285.28–35. [2] w iii 40.4.
[3] B vii 169.37. [4] B vii 165.13. [5] w iii 284.36.
[6] B v 265.37.

[7] This appealed to Goethe, who observed: 'Mathematics cannot eliminate prejudice, cannot mitigate wilfulness or allay partisanship; it can achieve nothing in the moral sphere.' Goethe, *Maximen und Reflexionen*, ed. Max Hecker (Weimar, 1907), No. 608 (p. 132).

[8] B v 264.36. [9] B vi 350.17.

[10] B ii 203.36, B i 378.7. Elsewhere Hamann refers to Spinoza as 'the Jewish flycatcher' (B vii 181.6).

exist in reality, as being more than a mere aid to stimulate attention – that leads into private fantasies. 'If *data* are given, why use *ficta?*'[1] To ask for them is to lose the fruit of the tree of life for that of (illusory) knowledge.[2] The passion of philosophers for abstractions leads to the reification of relations,[3] for example those of time and space. Time comes to us in the cadence of music, the rhythms of our heartbeat and of breathing,[4] and is directly perceptible, not 'a form of the understanding' as Kant would have it. Space is a relation between figures that we paint or draw, gestures and the like; each relation is a particular, and to generalise them is to create a network of fictions. Moreover, nothing is intelligible save in its relationships, for the world hangs by 'threads which cannot be sundered without hurting oneself or others',[5] and this can only be perceived in each concrete particular. To generalise this into a doctrine of terms versus relations, substances versus their attributes, is once again to barter reality for figments.

For Hamann reason disrupts and fragments; time, for instance, is reduced by it to isolated 'instants'. What gives them continuity is the 'thread' by means of which Providence – and it alone – unites them. This thread alone 'ensures the continuity of the moments and parts of the flow in a manner so powerful and indissoluble that it is all of one piece'.[6] If it were not for this our analytic reason would disintegrate our experience into the fictitious units of the natural sciences and be unable to reassemble them again. Hamann loves the English poets, for 'they don't analyse, they don't dissect'.[7] The English poet Dyer, for instance, writes about wool, whereas Lessing's fables are nothing but vapid philosophising.

Hamann's general trend is clear, but it is equally clear

---

[1] B vi 331.22. [2] B vi 492.9. [3] e.g. B vii 173.8 ff.
[4] w iii 286.17. [5] B iv 59.1. [6] w i 126.3.
[7] B ii 78.33.

that he suffers from genuine prejudice against the natural sciences as such. When Kant, in 1768, in the Königsberg garden of his friend the English merchant Green, said that astronomy had attained to such perfection that no new hypotheses were possible in it, Hamann felt he wanted to destroy the lot.[1] To constrict God and the infinite possibilities of his creation? Was it against inexhaustible divine – and rational – fertility that Kant marched out his army of abstractions? No general proposition, still less theories, can catch the variety and the concreteness of life. It may be that Hamann's hatred of science (which he admits) is in part due to the danger to his piety.[2] This is rationalised into a general onslaught on the cut and dried universe, without spontaneity, without surprises, without inexhaustible possibilities, any one of which, without rhyme or reason, might be realised. Hence the denunciation of determinism, because it seems to impose a man-made straitjacket upon the unclassifiable, upon God-Nature – that which every man, according to him, lives in and for, but which he cannot express, for to express is to use symbols, and symbols limit, abstract, cut reality into arbitrary slices, destroy it for the sake of trying to communicate the incommunicable.

The first task is to expose the deleterious influence of abstractions and the false knowledge which is built upon and out of them. This is the task of the modern Socrates, as Hamann conceives himself. There is something ironical, as he well knows, in representing Socrates, the great saint of the Enlightenment, the father of rationalism, the martyr to prejudice and tradition and religion, as the critic and indeed enemy of the new orthodoxy. Socrates was much written about in the eighteenth century, and cast in many roles: for some he is the father of critical enquiry, the enemy of superstition, traditional values, all that resists the methods of reason and logical argument, wherever this may

---

[1] B ii 416.29 ff.   [2] B ii 416.33 ff.

lead; for others he is principally a deist, or a freethinker; for still others he is a mystic guided by the inner voice of his 'daimon', which he is bound to follow in all his ways, or, again, an inspired precursor of Christianity (as he was to the Christian Platonists of the Renaissance, and, in a famous invocation, to Erasmus), or an early pietist in communion with his soul and its spiritual source, the Master of the universe, God himself. For Hamann Socrates is none of these avatars, but the opponent of the sophists, the gadfly of all the grand establishments, the fearless exposer of lies, hypocrisies, received opinions, delusions, all that is specious, clever, ingenious, the figments and fallacies of the arch-deceiver − the worldly, rootless intellect.[1] Helvétius and Voltaire, Descartes, Leibniz, Kant and Rousseau and Mendelssohn are the sophists of the present age. The first task of a man in pursuit of truth is to expose their hollow verbal fictions and declare that the task of reason is not the increase of theoretical knowledge − only the whole man, with his passions, emotions, desires, physiological reactions and all, can approach the truth − but the demonstration of the limits of knowledge, the exposure of man's ignorance and weakness.

This is what the *Socratic Memorabilia*, directed against the sophist Kant and the 'enlightened' merchant Berens, is meant to show. Socrates maddened the Athenians; Hamann is prepared to upset the bourgeoisie of Königsberg and Riga, to expose their *idées reçues*, to show that the official Christianity of the eighteenth century is nothing but paganism, that the real man of God is closer to thieves, beggars and

---

[1] Hamann knew something of Plato; but on Socrates he seems to have followed François Charpentier's *Life*, translated by Christian Thomasius. (Charpentier's 'La Vie de Socrate' was first published in his translation of Xenophon's *Memorabilia* in 1650, and revised more than once thereafter. Thomasius' 1693 translation was entitled *Das Ebenbild eines wahren und ohnpedantischen Philosophi, oder: Das Leben Socratis*; Hamann owned the second edition (Halle, 1720).)

criminals and to vagabonds and highwaymen – the irregulars of life – than to liberal Lutheran clergymen and rationalistic apologists for Christianity. A man of ironical doubt,
ironical humility, inner light, hypnotic genius, a middle
class *épateur* of all the bourgeois – this is Socrates, this is
Hamann.

The Enlightenment seems to Hamann an inversion of
natural values. In his diatribe against his friend F. K. von
Moser's *Master and Servant* of 1759 – a treatise in praise of
enlightened despotism – he identifies scientific method as
casuistry, Machiavellian manipulation of men; he conceives
the politics of enlightenment as a treatment of men as if
they were machines; he protests against the usurpation of
science, which has turned from a servant of man's fine and
infinite creative capacity into a dictator which determines
his position, morally, politically and personally.

Hamann does not offer a faculty for yielding propositions
superior to those of science – revealed truths, say, or the
axioms of natural law as conceived by either Aquinas or
Grotius. He opposes to scientific rules the empirical knowledge – practical rather than theoretical – which belongs to
any man who lives in a proper relationship to God and to
nature (what these are still remains to be seen). Words are
counters, he says, echoing Hobbes unconsciously; language
is a currency: men of genius can use it, but officials turn
it, as they turn everything, into a sterile dogmatism, which
they proceed to offer for their own and popular worship.
This turns human relations into mechanical ones, and makes
of what were living truths, or a spontaneous capacity for
acting in some appropriate fashion, a dead rule, an object
for idolatrous worship. This is a sermon against dehumanis-
ation and reification before those terms had been thought
of.

Hamann's great enemy is necessity – metaphysical or
scientific. Here he suspects that a specific human vision –
a moment of illumination or ordinary understanding, in

which a man grasped his situation and knew how to act, in order to achieve his spontaneously conceived ends – was turned into a pseudo-objective source of authority – a formula, a law, an institution, something outside men, conceived as eternal, unalterable, universal; a world of necessary truths, mathematics, theology, politics, physics, which man did not make and cannot alter, crystalline, pure, an object of divine worship for atheists. He rejects this absolutely. No bridge is needed between necessary and contingent truths because the laws of the world in which man lives are as contingent as the 'facts' in it. All that exists could have been otherwise if God had so chosen, and can be so still. God's creative powers are unlimited, man's are limited; nothing is eternally fixed, at least nothing in the human world – outside it we know nothing, at any rate in this life. The 'necessary' is relatively stable, the 'contingent' is relatively changing, but this is a matter of degree, not kind.

Any attempt to introduce a deep division between types of cognition or types of entities – any kind of dualism between 'reality' and 'appearance' – seems to him plain denial of the unity of experience and an escape into mythology. In this respect he is with the empiricist positivists against orthodox religion and the central tradition of Western metaphysics; the union of mysticism and empiricism as against rationalism here emerges in full strength for perhaps the first time. Hamann is a genuine nominalist, as is made clear in his theory of language. Hence his violent opposition to the notion that there is a world of eternal essences connected internally by logical relationships, or ontological bonds; a world whose bony structure an ideally clear language could mirror – as Leibniz certainly, and perhaps Descartes, believed. He rejects the very notion of an essence from which necessary characteristics or – still more insane – a necessary past and a necessary future could in principle be deduced. The world for him consists of persons and things and their *de facto* relationships, and the only evidence for them is experience, outside which there is nothing, save that such experience for him not merely includes but has as its very centre the relationship of man and God.

He pursues the devil of dualism wherever he sees it, and in his earliest writings he uses Hume's strict empiricism to destroy alleged necessary connections in nature together with their metaphysical guarantees and special non-empirical paths towards their discovery. Later he applies the very same method to refuting rationalist politics and ethics, for example in Mendelssohn's or Lessing's attempts to divide one aspect of human life from another, say religion from civil law, 'inner' from 'outer' conduct, the State from the Church, and the like.

Mendelssohn's chief purpose in the work that Hamann attacked, *Jerusalem: A Plea for the Toleration of the Jews*, was to found both moral and political obligation on natural law and natural rights, which were to be distinguished from less perfect rights and less stringent laws and duties, as they developed in civil society. The specific points against Mendelssohn are of little interest now: the whole framework in which the debate was conducted has become largely obsolete. But what is characteristic is Hamann's indignation with Mendelssohn for supposing that man is a compound of reason and feeling who can be analysed into his individual ingredients, so that one can say that as a human being he has certain natural rights and duties, as a citizen other rights and other duties; that, for instance, the rights of man *qua* man, say to any religious opinions he may hold, cannot be cut into by his duties as a citizen, say to obey the government in the public sphere, which, *ex hypothesi*, must not impinge upon the private domain. These divisions – what a man owes God and what he owes Caesar, the 'public' and the 'private' – seemed to Hamann a fatal method of cutting human beings to pieces, like so much inanimate flesh. Man for him is one: feeling shapes belief and belief feeling. If religion is to be taken seriously at all it must penetrate every aspect of a man's life; if it is true, it is the heart and soul of a man's being; a religion that is confined to its 'proper' sphere – like an official with limited powers, to be kept in its place, not allowed to interfere – that is a mockery. Better deny religion altogether, like an atheist, than reduce it to a tame and harmless exercise within an artificially demarcated zone that it must not transgress.

Hamann's entire conception of Christian society rests on a passionate belief in the opposite of all this – that man is one and that if God (as he believed) not only exists but enters into every fibre, every nook and cranny, of human experience, the notion of confining him to his 'sphere', of creating frontiers against his worship, is a blasphemy and self-deception. If this leads to confusion of private and public, to interference and intolerance, Hamann does not mind at all: toleration of differences is a denial of their importance. Man is one, with all the uncomfortable consequences that this carries; attempts to show that all beliefs that continue to contribute to 'peace', 'harmony', 'rationality' – whether religious, political or any other – are to be encouraged by the secular State (as advocated for example by Spinoza, Lessing and, in effect, the French utilitarians, Helvétius and Co.) seem to him tantamount to a denial that beliefs – truth – matter much. All efforts to demarcate the private from the public, the inner from the outer, contingent from necessary (here he mistakenly holds Kant to be particularly guilty – the mere words 'pure reason' infuriated Hamann, who misrepresented the *Critique of Pure Reason* to a quite fantastic degree), seemed to him nothing but efforts to evade reality, to label and classify various aspects of it and invent imaginary attributes and functions for them, intended to save men from the agony of being (as a later philosophy was to call it) 'authentic', of truly understanding themselves and their relations to others. All philosophical spectacles are for Hamann distorting lenses – efforts at escape from reality into the security of a theory from which the tangled avenues of real life have been kept out.

In a sense the great polemic against Mendelssohn and the humanistic liberals of Berlin reveals Hamann's position – at any rate as it was after his conversion in London – more vividly than even his more obviously theological writings. Mendelssohn is a characteristic representative of the Enlightenment, sincere, rational, humane, unoriginal, moderate, and exceptionally clear. Every one of these qualities irritated Hamann – even sincerity allied to a calm and conciliatory temper – for he believed that in serious matters detachment, dispassionate judgement, an attempt to do justice to opposite sides of the case, were merely a cloak for timidity and indifference. Theory for him was practice, and practice was the exercise of will, the self-commitment to what one not merely recognised but felt and, in a sense, willed to be true with every fibre of one's being in the perpetual battle for the word of God, for its realisation on earth – or against it. Indifference to this – suspension of judgement, coolness – is a contemptible aspect of failure to face reality.

Mendelssohn expounded the orthodox liberal doctrine of natural law, according to which the State was founded upon reciprocal promises or compacts between the ruler and the ruled, each to fulfil his proper, stipulated functions, and rested on the sanctity of promises, as ordained by natural law, recognised by all rational men – the law claiming universal obedience. He drew from this the normal liberal consequence, drawn by Spinoza before him, that since the promise was valid only if freely given, it entailed freedom of thought and expression, the absence of coercion towards men's beliefs, including their recognition of natural law, upon which the validity of promises was founded; for unless men were free to arrive at whatever conclusions were indicated by the operation of natural reason, the very notions of natural law and the obligations that sprang from it, and of a rational basis for government, could not be realised. While a government might have the right and duty to restrain or coerce action, it could not, without destroying the foundations of its own rights, dictate belief or persecute non-conformity which did not take violent forms or seek to disturb public order. This was the eighteenth-century distillation from the views of religious dissent in the seventeenth century held by Spinoza, Locke and all the fathers of the liberal enlightenment.

Hamann would have none of this. Everything in it seemed to him false: the notion of natural law, the notion that the State or any other human institution rested on some intellectual act of assent, for example a promise, seemed to him absurd. To keep one's word is to act normally as a thinking, feeling being. Society rests on this as a natural phenomenon.[1] The State was a form of human association that grew from natural needs which themselves could not be explained but were part of the general mystery of creation, that is, the mystery of why things were as they were and not otherwise – something that God had not chosen to reveal to us in any detail. God had spoken to men in manifold ways: through history, through nature, through Holy Writ – his words revealed by his prophets and by his only begotten Son.

To be a man was to understand in some degree what one's goal on earth was – this one understood only by understanding oneself, which one could do only in that human intercourse in which men were mirrors of one another, in which by understanding others – by communication – and by being understood by them, I understood myself; for if I were alone in the world, communication, and therefore speech, and therefore thought (which for Hamann were one), could never develop. Therefore the existence of a

---

[1] w iii 300.27 ff., 301.25 ff.

49

complex web of human relations was presupposed by the very possibility of thought, and did not need its products as its justification. Indeed, it needed no justification at all: it was a given fact to be accepted on pain of ignoring reality, and so being driven into error and madness.

Hamann thought that the notion of justifying society – or for that matter the State – was as absurd as the attempt to justify the existence of speech, or love or art, or the existence of plants and animals in the world. Why should I obey the king, or indeed anyone? Not because I promised – this is neither historically true nor logically required, for why did I promise? For the sake of happiness? But that is not what I seek on this earth – only Frenchmen and utilitarians seek this (his tone at such points greatly resembles that of Nietzsche, especially on the English). It is because I am a man and seek to fulfil all my powers – to live, create, worship, understand, love, hate, eat, drink, procreate – in the way that I was created to do, and if I stumble and err I have but to read the Bible or study human history or look at nature to see what it is that God's creatures are meant to do; for there are parables and allegories everywhere around me. The story of Abraham, the story of Ruth, may be the story of an oriental patriarch or a Moabite woman, but they are also the stories of every man and every woman. Similarly, there are events in the history of my community, and there are phenomena in the nature that surrounds me, all of which are ways in which the Creator speaks to me, darkly sometimes, but in the end in such a manner that even the meanest soul can get some inkling of it – telling me what I am, what I can be, how to realise myself, not along paths logically deducible from contemplating my imaginary essence, but by understanding my relationship to God and to the world. This relationship can be realised only in action, in the actual act of living, in pursuing ends, in hurling myself against obstacles; the proper direction, the right things to do, faith alone can supply – that faith without which Hume could not eat an egg or drink a glass of water, without which there is for us no external world, no past, no awareness of objects or persons; that faith which cannot itself be bolstered by rational considerations, for it generates reason and is not generated by it; it is itself presupposed in every act of consciousness, and therefore cannot itself be justified, for it is that which justifies everything else.

So much for promises as the basis of political obligation. Natural law was for Hamann an equally hideous chimera, a great bleak construction of the rationalising intellect which has no reality at all. The word of God – faith – that saved him in London during the darkest hours of his life speaks differently to different men in different circumstances. There is no single, universal, public, objective structure – natural law or the rational structure of the universe, or anything else invented by philosophers – which can be contemplated by anyone at any time, and, provided he has adequate intellectual power, can be perceived in its immutable, eternal essence and authority. The whole of the rationalist construction of the Berlin sages seems to him a denial of activity, variety, energy, life, faith, God, and man's unique relation to him. And into his diatribe there enters, as one might expect, a note of personal violence, hatred of *raisonneurs*, heretics, and, as was not unusual, Jews.[1]

---

[1] Hamann's attitude to the Jews has been the subject of some dispute. See, for example, the essay by Ze'ev Levy on Hamann's controversy with Mendelssohn in Bernhard Gajek and Albert Meier (eds), *Johann Georg Hamann und die Krise der Aufklärung* (Frankfurt am Main etc., 1990), pp. 327–44. However, there is undoubtedly a scattering of anti-Jewish remarks in Hamann's writings (see, for example, w iii 146.34, 151.31, 395.11, 397.18; B vii 181.6, 467.26; as well as several passages in *Golgotha und Scheblimini!*); and although he was certainly concerned to defend what he saw as true Judaism against perversions of it, and well disposed to Mendelssohn as an individual, it is not plausible to maintain that he was free of what later came to be called anti-Semitism. In this he was, of course, entirely typical of his age.

Mendelssohn had been a friend, in some sense a patron; nevertheless, Hamann is no more reluctant than other writers of his time and milieu – among them, at times, Kant, surprisingly enough – to denounce the materialistic, rationalistic unrealism and arrogant authority of anti-Christian liberal culture, a conception of a self-appointed élite of frozen dogmatists. He denounces Berlin as dominated by secular, liberal culture, positive, critical, atheist, analytical, disruptive; this note is to be found later in Maistre and in the entire anti-rationalist, anti-Semitic literature of the nineteenth century, until it finally reaches a point of violent hysteria in Austro-German racism and National Socialism. Jews, Wolffians, materialistic dwellers in the modern Babylon[1] – all are one to Hamann. The Jews emerge as the eternal critics, the detached, uncommitted judges of the Christian world. To tolerate them as an organised religion is a concession to that liberalism and rationalism that constitutes a denial of what men are for, to serve the true God, hear his words and feel and will and act them in every moment of their life on earth; this is known better to the common people than to the alienated wiseacres who dominate politics and intellectual life – the tame philosophers at the courts of the enlightened despot. Hence again the combination of obscurantism, populism, fideism and anti-intellectualism, faith in the common people and hatred of natural science and criticism that was to have so powerful and so fatal an influence in the two centuries that followed.

Hamann's vision is that of human beings as children, to whom their father speaks, and who learn everything at his knee – much as his own ideas were intelligible to him only in terms of his own childhood, of the Bible that was at the centre of his pietist upbringing, and to which in moments of crisis and despair he constantly returned. Men must often

---

[1] See w iii 397.18.

be conceived of as deaf children whom one must painfully make repeat certain words whose very sound they cannot apprehend.[1] If they are docile they will never 'oppose their nature to their reason and of their habits make a necessity',[2] and so generate that dualism of nature, instinct, sense of kinship with others and with natural objects versus sceptical analytical individualising reason; or of creature versus creator; or of natural versus supernatural or anti-natural;[3] or of necessary versus contingent.

What is this category of nature and the natural to which French materialists are constantly appealing? Uniformities amongst the phenomena? But what guarantees have we of their continuance? Only God's will. 'What is there in nature, in the commonest of natural phenomena, that is not, for us, a miracle in the most precise sense of the term?'[4] It is a miracle because the causal nexus in terms of which we distinguish the normal and the miraculous is nothing but a fiction of our own making, a device, and not (as Hamann delights in saying that Hume pointed out) something that corresponds to reality, to an object of observation, or feeling, or any other direct apprehension on our part. From this he develops a view that is close to the occasionalism of Malebranche and Berkeley, and is one of the streams that fed those romantic philosophers who saw reality not as dead matter obeying unaltering laws but as a self-generating process, a thrusting forward of a living will – blind and unconscious in Schelling and Schopenhauer and Bergson, progressively attaining to greater and greater self-consciousness in the metaphysical systems of Hegel and Marx (whether in spiritual-cultural development, or in that of the more material struggle against nature or other men) or to the realisation of divine purpose that is intrinsic to the will of God, as in the metaphysics of the Christian religion.

[1] w i 14.19.   [2] w i 24.25.   [3] w i 24.27 ff.
[4] w i 24.30.

Reason is said by the secular philosophers to be one and the same in all men: but this is not so, else there would not have been so many conflicting philosophies all claiming to be justified by the same faculty of reason. The only unitary source of truth is of course revelation – reason or the conflict of rationalisms has led to the Tower of Babel, which was laid in ruins; only when God descended to us and was made flesh was the possibility of a unitary faith made possible. This God is certainly not the abstraction of the deists, but creative and passionate – above all a person who speaks to us through history and nature, a person capable of being loved and worshipped, not the abstract unity and harmony of, say, Shaftesbury or Mendelssohn and his Christian friends. This is certainly, as Jean Blum says, the God of popular consciousness, not the shadowy deity of abstract thought. He adds: 'Hamann's thought is what those who do not normally think would think if they did think.'[1]

Since Hamann fervently believed in a personal God who made the heaven and the earth and governed them in accordance with his own will, he was a teleologist, but not a rationalistic one, still less an optimistic utilitarian. The three concepts that dominate him are those of creation, intentionality and its correlative, understanding. To understand is to understand someone; things or events or facts as such cannot be understood, only noted or described; by themselves they do not speak to us, they do not pursue purposes, they do not act or want or strive, they merely occur, are, exist – and come to be and pass away. To understand is to understand a voice speaking, or if not a voice, something else that conveys meaning, that is, the use of something – a sound, a patch of colour, a movement – to refer to, or stand for, something else. If we can claim to understand history, we can only mean by this that we understand not merely what occurred – that is mere

---

[1] op. cit. (p. 10 above, note 2), pp. 47–8.

transcription — but why, with what end in view; not merely what things are, but what they are at; and if they — the inanimate objects, say — are not at anything, are just a succession in a causal chain, events occurring in a certain identifiable order, then to say that we understand them must mean that we understand what those who produced them, consciously or unconsciously, intended them for; if nobody intended them for anything — if they just occurred for no reason — there is no understanding them, the category of understanding is inapplicable. But of course in history we understand the purposes of agents, not merely individuals who are fully conscious of what they are pursuing, and some among them who are aware of why they are pursuing it — but also groups of human beings, cultures, nations, Churches, which may be said to pursue collective purposes, although the analysis of this notion is far from easy. Hamann had no doubt that different civilisations pursued different ends and had a different conception of the world, which was part and parcel of their ways of life, that is, of the civilisations that they were; and this notion he transmitted to Herder, who, apparently without the benefit of Vico's ideas — similar to his own and in some respects more original and profound — played a major part in transforming the human sciences and men's ideas about themselves.

But what, in that case, is nature, both as we contemplate it in ordinary life, as it forms the subject of sciences, and as, in interplay with active agents, it enters the web of human history as the weft to which the human agent is the warp? If the notion of understanding nature is to make any sense, it can only be because it too is at something, intends, strives, acts; or else is that whereby others do so. Hamann was not a pantheist. He was not an animist of any kind. He did not believe in active powers in stones or trees either as part of some omnipresent divinity or as independent centres of purposive action, as the pagans did. He believed in a personal deity, who created the world for his own often inscrutable purpose. To this degree he stands with the teleologists – Aristotle, Aquinas, Hegel. Where he sharply parts company from them is in denying that the divine (or cosmic) purpose is necessarily rational, that his relation to the universe is – even if in an infinitely higher degree or sense – identical with that of any earthly planner, whose reason is definable as a disposition towards thought in accordance with the laws of logic, the fitting of means to ends in accordance with proven principles, whether derived a priori or empirically, the test of which is consistency, systematic unity, generality and the like. This appears to him to attribute to God our own poor categories – poor in comparison with an infinity of ways that could exist in which an agent could act and not be capable of being caught in the net of our particular intellectual equipment. Since God exists, everything that he makes embodies his purpose; but to attempt to deduce his existence from the behaviour of the created world seems to him a particularly degraded kind of anthropomorphism – the notion that God is like a mathematician or an architect or some other kind of rational practitioner is an arbitrary and blasphemous assumption.

Hamann is strongly prejudiced against reason and the sciences, which seem to him to afford a poverty-stricken view even of human possibilities. The meaning of action for him is better exemplified in the infinitely various and rich world of individual self-expression: the effort of children to represent things to themselves and to communicate desires and fantasies, to express their personalities by creating works of art that convey their vision – that is, convey meaning by using primitive scrawls, or something not identical with themselves, to represent what they imagine or conceive to exist and to be worth identifying. What children do is in principle the same as that which all men do, from the simplest bodily gesture or scratch on the wall of a cave to the most sophisticated and profound spiritual expression in art, philosophy, literature, religion – identical, too, with entire styles of life through which nations and Churches and cultures express themselves.

God is inscrutable. But Hamann thought that if there was a key it was not in conceiving nature as a rational system from any part of which deductions could be made to any other part, following therein the divine logic of the plan on which it was constructed. He saw no evidence of this. The key for him was in understanding; that is, in having revealed to one what the Creator meant to convey. If we understand other human beings by having it revealed to us what a given set of marks on paper or sounds or artistic representation is meant to express or say – however this may happen, and this Hamann regards as always somewhat mysterious – then we must, to the extent of our powers, understand God's meaning by viewing his creation in this way.

It can come closer to us than that. In the Bible, Hamann believes, our Father spoke to us directly. We can only understand as much of this as we are capable of embracing within the particular concepts and categories of meaning that happen to have fallen to our lot as human beings, as Germans, as citizens of Königsberg; we can expand our powers by learning other languages, other styles of art, anything but the dead, artificial symbolism – the technical terminology of the sciences – that springs for him from no rich, imaginative source, and does not convey purpose and life in a sufficiently human fashion. Why should what God intends necessarily fit into our narrow, rational categories? It is at least a wider and more generous analogy – even if all analogies are inadequate – to assume him to be an artist whose purposes are manifold to a literally infinite extent; intelligible, understandable, only as we understand art, each concrete expression by itself as an individual whole, not as a link in some mechanical or logical system that a machine could operate, that one needs no imagination to comprehend. We understand nature as we understand art, as perpetual divine creation, in accordance with patterns that may illuminate divine purpose for us in some apparently remote field. A proper understanding of nature, the tracing of the divine purpose, however feebly and uncertainly, may cast light upon divine purpose in history, in my own individual life, or anywhere else.

This is Hamann's world: the union of the naïvely simple conception of God as the omnipotent Eternal Father, to whom I am bound by relations of awe and love and total dependence — perhaps the most widespread and primitive of all human attitudes — with a theory of creation, meaning, understanding that is by no means simple, and a full grasp of which created the humanities as we know them today, a late and sophisticated product of the human consciousness; together with the dogma that everything is created, that is, intended to do or stand for something by its creator — since if to assume that reason can unravel what an artist, or a lover, or an ordinary man in ordinary circumstances does and means is absurd, how much more is this so when applied to God. Where there is creation, there can always be revelation.[1]

Philosophy claims to be the explanation of life, but 'life is action',[2] not a static thing to be analysed like a botanist's specimen. An action cannot be described in the categories

---

[1] Of course there is much else in Hamann's conception of God. He is not only the poet who creates the world from the beginning, but also 'the thief at the end of days' (w ii 206.20; cf. Revelation 16: 15), that is, the final judge of all that he has made and now takes unto himself. Moreover he not only compassionately descended to the level of his creations, but displayed divine humility in the Incarnation — *forma servi*, as a mode of revelation. And his unity embraces opposites — infinite calm with infinite energy (w ii 204.10) — the *coincidentia oppositorum* of which Cusanus had spoken is of his essence. This is Hamann's theology, but far more striking is his doctrine of the relation of God to his creatures.

[2] B iv 288.29.

provided by the Cartesians, or even the Lockeans and Leibnizians, for all their talk of movement and change. The task of true philosophy is to explain[1] life in all its contradictions, with all its peculiarities; not to smooth it out or substitute for it 'castles in the air'[2] – harmonious, tidy, beautiful and false.

The first place in which to look is that which is most familiar to me – myself. 'Self-knowledge and self-love is the true norm of our knowledge of men and our love of men.'[3] All our desires and longings seek for self-understanding as their object. The desire to know ourselves as we are and to be ourselves, and accept no substitutes – by the 'descent to Hell'[4] of self-knowledge – is the foundation of our entire activity.[5] 'Do not forget, for the sake of the *cogito*, the noble *sum*.'[6] Expel metaphysics, like Hagar,[7] and what do we discover in ourselves? Desire and passion and faith, which our heart sometimes seeks to satisfy with lies, for it is a born liar.[8] To suppress what we find in favour of the apotheosis of only one of our faculties – capacity for rational analysis – is a self-mutilation which can only lead to a perversion of our nature and distortion of the truth. Flesh has been given us, and passions; they do not sin by existing; they can be perverted, but the seducer is always cold reason, which desires to assert its own authority and usurp that of the other faculties.

Mystical rationalism despises the flesh and seeks to substitute for God's creation something of its own: that is what the Greeks sought to do at Eleusis. Philosophic rationalism is at a still further remove, a feeble substitute for the mystical variety. It preaches self-reliance, the attempt to construct the universe out of resources provided by logic, geometry, chemistry, and the other collections of useful

---

[1] w ii 199.1.   [2] B v 265.37.   [3] B iv 6.20.
[4] 'Höllenfahrt', w ii 164.17.   [5] w iv 424.47.
[6] B vi 230.35.   [7] B vi 231.12.
[8] B i 297.12. St Paul was Hamann's favourite apostle.

figments that seek to substitute themselves for the direct vision of reality. Nothing is so insufficient for this purpose as reason. We are compounded of desires and passions as well as reason: our proper function is to learn from history, nature and God, their creator, and to create ourselves. Young had said that not only reason, but the passions too, have been sanctified by baptism. We must create with the whole of ourselves, not only our brains but the entire organic whole.

Hamann's prose is full of reiteration of words like 'mutilation' and 'castration'. 'How can a man who has mutilated his organs feel?'[1] Bacon is quoted in the same passage as charging philosophers with mutilating nature by their abstractions. Passions are like limbs.[2] To maim them is to deprive us of the power not only of sensation but of understanding.[3] Philosophy can control and guide, but never initiate.[4] All energy is psycho-physical: it proceeds from the unity of body and soul. To tame the passions is to weaken spontaneity and genius. How then are vicious consequences to be avoided? By faith – self-surrender into the arms of Providence. Since God was made flesh this does not crush our body or passions. Sensualism in Hamann is combined with self-surrender; the abandonment of the latter leads to arid atheism, of the former to equally arid puritanism. Spontaneity is compatible with self-surrender but not with system.

Condillac wrote a treatise on sensations, in which Hamann, towards the end of his life, took some interest, but it is precisely such careful positivists as Condillac that he most detests, if only because they do not delve into the depths and splendours of the ravaged human soul, because they seek to make of nature an elegant front garden. (Goethe later claimed to be liberated from shallow classicism of this type by Herder, who in fact preached to him, at Strasburg, doctrines put forward by Hamann.) Modern writers have

---

[1] w ii 206.1.   [2] B i 442.32.   [3] w ii 206.1.
[4] w ii 162.33.

turned the savage violence of the Beasts of the Apocalypse into Lessing's harmless moral imagery, and Aesop's fierce vision into smooth Horatian elegance. To understand truly one must descend to the depths of the orgies, to Bacchus and Ceres.[1] Nieuwentyt's and Newton's and Buffon's discoveries cannot inspire poetry as mythology has done. For this there must be a reason.[2] Nature has been killed by the rationalists because they deny the senses and the passions. 'Passion alone gives to abstractions and hypotheses hands, feet, wings; images it endows with spirit, life, language. Where are swifter arguments to be found? Where the rolling thunder of eloquence, and its companion, the monosyllabic brevity of lightning?'[3] For this we must go to the artist, not to the modern philosopher; to the Bible and to Luther, not to the Greeks; to Milton, not to the French versifiers.[4]

If we are to pray for the whole of ourselves and avoid the fate of poor Origen or Abelard — austerity, dry intellectualism, passionless contemplation, self-castration are associated into one symbolic pattern in his mind — then we must not suppress our 'lower' nature: it was given to us by God as surely as all else. 'I have always sought to identify and pick out the *inferna* of a torso, rather than the *superna* of a bust,' he wrote to Herder late in life; '. . . my coarse imagination has never been able to picture a creative spirit without *genitalia*.'[5] Why are the glorious organs of generation objects of shame? One must not speak of general human sentiment on this subject; it does not exist; '*children* are not full of

---

[1] W ii 201.4 ff.   [2] W ii 205.20.

[3] W ii 208.20; 'monosyllabic' because the German for lightning is 'Blitz'.

[4] Such passages are reminiscent of Burke's famous essay on the sublime and beautiful. Hamann certainly read Burke: and there is an affinity, particularly in the paean to the sublime as compared to the classically perfect. But the parallel should not be pressed too far. Joseph de Maistre, whose attacks on the French Enlightenment are not dissimilar, is unlikely ever to have heard of Hamann.

[5] B ii 415.20.

prudery, nor *savages*, nor Cynic philosophers'.[1] Prudery is
an inherited piece of morality – habit, due to consensus.
And consensus is for Hamann the worst of authorities,
appeal to good sense, tame middle-class sentiment, against
the thunder of God and revelation. 'If the passions are mere
pudenda, do they therefore cease to be the tools of virility?'[2]
And again, 'the *pudenda* of our organisms are so closely
united to the secret depths of our *heart* and *brain* that a
total rupture of this natural union is impossible'.[3] To divide
the flesh from the spirit is to blaspheme against God, who
created us one. The truth is revealed to us in the Bible
because the story is so simple, sincere and realistic, because
it is childishly naïve, and so a true embodiment of human
life. Since children are not ashamed of their bodies as the
civilised man of the eighteenth century is, in this sense too
we must take Christ's words literally and seek to restore
within ourselves the less broken, more spontaneous view of
life to be found among the innocent, those not bedevilled
by doctrine or a despotic social organisation of enlightened
autocrats either in politics or in the sciences or the arts.

Hamann's anti-rationalism, his emphasis on the fullness of
life, and in particular on the importance of everything in
man that is generative, creative, passionate – the sexual
metaphors, the sensuality of his imagination at its most
inspired and religious – have a clear affinity with the views
of William Blake. When Blake says 'Without Contraries
is no progression. Attraction and Repulsion, Reason and
Energy, Love and Hate, are necessary to Human existence',[2]
that is pure Hamann. So is

[1] w iii 199.28.   [2] w ii 208.11.   [3] b v 167.16.
[2] *The Marriage of Heaven and Hell*, plate 3. The text followed in
these quotations from Blake is that to be found in *William Blake's
Writings*, ed. G. E. Bentley, Jr (Oxford, 1978). References to this
edition are given in parentheses, by volume and page, at the end of
the relevant notes, thus: (i 77).

> Lo! A shadow of horror is risen
> In Eternity! Unknown, Unprolific?
> Self-closd, all-repelling . . .
> Brooding secret, the dark power hid.[1]

The 'shadow of horror' is of course the 'Spectre', that is, cold reason, arid, hard, with lust for dominion, mad pride, ambitious, violent, hating, brutally and implacably egoistic, perverted, avid, as against the 'Emanation', which is tender, loving and creative. 'The Spectre is the Reasoning Power in Man';[2] 'The Spectre is, in Giant Man: insane';[3] 'An Abstract objecting power that negatives every thing',[4] 'brutish Deform'd . . . a ravening devouring lust continually Craving & devouring'.[5] This echoes Hamann's very analogous sentiments. So does the contrast between 'Imagination the real & eternal World' as against the 'Vegetable Universe'[6] of ordinary life and the 'Vegetable Glass of Nature'.[7]

Blake differs from Hamann in regarding the external world as 'Dirt upon my feet, No part of me',[8] and in his general anti-empiricism, but the Spectre's boast − 'Am I not Bacon & Newton & Locke . . . my two wings: Voltaire: Rousseau?'[9] − is much in Hamann's tradition. So is the hatred of man-made laws, laws needed to fence men off:

> And their children wept, & built
> Tombs in the desolate places,
> And form'd laws of prudence, and call'd them
> The eternal laws of God.[10]

[1] *The First Book of Urizen*, plate 3, lines 1−3, 7 (i 241).
[2] *Jerusalem*, plate 74, line 10 (i 581).
[3] ibid., plate 37, line 4 (i 495).
[4] ibid., plate 10, line 14 (i 434).
[5] *Vala*, p. 84, lines 38−9 (ii 1196).
[6] *Jerusalem*, plate 77 (i 587).
[7] 'Vision of the Last Judgement', p. 69d (ii 1010).
[8] ibid., p. 95 (ii 1027).
[9] *Jerusalem*, plate 54, lines 17−18 (i 352).
[10] *The First Book of Urizen*, plate 28, lines 4−7 (i 282).

This is precisely Hamann's doctrine. So is the thunder against asceticism: 'Men are admitted into Heaven not because they have Curbed & governd their Passions or have No Passions but because they have Cultivated Their Understandings. The Treasures of Heaven are not Negations of Passion.'[1] And Hamann would have had profound sympathy for

> That they may call a shame & sin
> Loves Temple that God dwelleth in
> And hide in Secret hidden Shrine
>   The Naked Human form divine
> And render that a Lawless thing
>   On which the Soul Expands its wing.[2]

and

> Children of the future Age,
> Reading this indignant page;
> Know that in a former time,
> Love! sweet Love! was thought a crime.[3]

or for what he says in *Jerusalem*: 'I am not a God afar off, I am a brother and a friend . . . Lo! we are One.'[4] He is still closer to Hamann in his passionate defence of free will against all forms of determinism, and in his doctrine of salvation through art, which he identified with a vision of God, until he arrived at the equation Christian = Artist. And 'Jesus & his Apostles & Disciples were all Artists';[5] this in sharp contrast to the Greek view of life, which for

---

[1] 'Vision of the Last Judgement', p. 87z (ii 1024).

[2] 'The Everlasting Gospel', p. 50 (ii 1060).

[3] *Songs of Experience*, plate 51 ('A Little GIRL Lost'), lines 1–4 (i 196).

[4] *Jerusalem*, plate 4, lines 18, 20 (i 422).

[5] 'Laocoon', aphorism 16 (i 665).

Blake was rational, scientific, secular, blind. Finally, nothing is more Hamannian than 'Art is the Tree of Life . . . Science is the Tree of Death.'[1] D. H. Lawrence would have agreed.

As for Blake's political views and his mystical anarchism, that is another matter. Hamann, despite all his objections to the King of Prussia, was in the end a German and a Prussian – more the latter than the former, as he indefatigably points out to Herder, whom he suspects of abandoning Prussia for Germany.[2] In part, this is to be explained by the fact that they were both influenced by Böhme, a child of East German culture, and Blake by Swedenborg, who lived in a climate of opinion not unlike that of Hamann in northern Europe.

The close connection of the notion of free creation with sexual fertility – and indeed of religious with sexual imagery – is familiar enough. Like Blake, Hamann identifies reason with repression. He was himself a sensual man and took pride in the fullness of his life. The unity of theory and practice was not a mere abstract doctrine for him: he genuinely detested anything that confined the human spirit, all rules and regulations as such. They were perhaps necessary, but if so they were necessary evils. Rules, he says, returning to his favourite field of metaphor, are like Vestal Virgins: only because a Vestal was violated did Rome acquire a population,[3] and if rules are not violated there is

---

[1] ibid., aphorisms 17, 19 (i 665, 666).

[2] For example: 'You pride yourself on being a German and are ashamed of being a Prussian, which is still ten times better' (B ii 434.5). Compare this remark in a letter to Kriegrath Scheffner: 'I have scarcely any desire to be a German . . . I am nothing more or less than an East Prussian' (B v 199.15). I owe these quotations to Gunnar Beck.

[3] 'Rules are vestal virgins who populated Rome, thanks to the exceptions which they perpetuated.' W ii 345.11. Romulus and Remus were the children by Mars of Rhea Silvia, a Vestal Virgin.

no issue; one must have rules but also break them.[1] Hagedorn says, 'We don't judge painters by the exceptions.'[2] Hamann answers: 'We poor readers do; for us, all the masterpieces in a cabinet of paintings are exceptions. He who cannot produce an exception cannot produce a masterpiece.'[3]

Passages in this vein, painstakingly collected by Hamann's exceedingly erudite student Rudolf Unger, are usually held to be only symptoms of his own richly sensual imagination. But they are far more than this: they are a passionate protest against what he regarded as the insane rationalism of the Enlightenment, the fact that, despite its professed empiricism, it did not pay sufficient attention to the irrational factors in man, whether in their normal or abnormal manifestations. The erotic writers – Crébillon, Parny and the like – trivialised the passions even further; the writings of the Marquis de Sade were not taken seriously at that time; nor did Diderot's remarkable explorations of sexual conduct attract much notice, even among the *philosophes*. Rousseau, whose influence was far wider, was prudish and morbidly puritanical about such matters. If he described them it was in a violent desire to confess, to draw attention to himself and his inescapable vices, and his passionate candour and freedom from hypocrisy. Hamann, and after him Blake, were among the few writers before the romantics who conceived the doctrine of the need for total self-expression as the object of the natural human craving for freedom, and wrote about it without excitement or terror, and with profound and sympathetic insight. The liberation of writers like Goethe and Schiller, Shelley and Wordsworth, even Hugo, from the despotism – moral as well as aesthetic – of the laws of fanatical eighteenth-century

[1] w ii 362.16 ff.
[2] C. L. von Hagedorn, *Betrachtungen über die Mahlerey* (Leipzig, 1762), vol. 1, p. 150; quoted by Hamann at w ii 345.4.
[3] w ii 345.9.

rationalism ultimately sprang from the revolt, which in this case took a religious form, against the enemies of man's unbroken nature.

The principal enemies for Hamann were Kant and Helvétius. Kant he accused of 'old, cold prejudice in favour of mathematics',[1] of a *'gnostic* hatred of matter' and a *'mystical* love of form',[2] though it is Helvétius (who was widely read in Germany) who preaches the shallow eudaemonism (*Glückseligkeitslehre*) which is the curse of Germany in his day. At least Rousseau and Diderot recognise the existence of spiritual conflict within man. Helvétius, who believes that public utility is all in all; that justice is public interest supported by power; that private honesty is of little importance to society, since vices can be harnessed as successfully to the public interest as virtues; that virtue without the support of public power is a pitiful absurdity; that to love the good for its own sake is as impossible as to love evil for its own sake; that the 'thermometer' of public evaluation of morals constantly alters,[3] hence absolute values are a conception absurd in itself; that genius is a product of artificial culture, and a reformed education can breed it as often and as much as may be needed by the society of the future; that personal liberty, if it is an obstacle to the rational organisation of society, may be suppressed – this man is Hamann's natural enemy. Everything is false here: the psychology, the scale of values, the notion of what man's nature is, the total blindness to man's inner life, or the abysses of which Augustine and Pascal, Dante and Luther wrote, and which Helvétius and his friends blandly dismiss as an irrational aberration to be cured by a competent physician or 'engineer of human souls'.

Hamann is furiously angry and, as was often the case

---

[1] w iii 285.18.   [2] w iii 285.15.

[3] *De l'esprit*, essay 1, chapter 7: p. 116 in *Oeuvres complètes de M. Helvétius*, vol. 1 (Liège, 1774); cf. essay 2, chapter 13.

with other, particularly later, exasperated enemies of the triumphant march of science, falls into bitter and savage obscurantism: freethinkers are a danger not merely to sound religion, but to morals, to public order; they are inciters to political mutiny. The reference of everything to *bon sens* is in effect dangerous subjectivism: it offers the views of a group of atheists as an infallible criterion.[1] *'Obedience to reason . . . is a call to open rebellion.'*[2] The bonds of subordination are broken, subordination becomes impossible, if reason is not submissive and denied.[3] Authority must be one and not many. It resides not in reason but in paradox, absurdity, in what is 'foolishness to the Greeks'.[4] (This is echoed by Kierkegaard in the following century.) There cannot be any peace between faith and reason. So far from religion being reason *in excelsis* as Thomism teaches, one must make up one's mind either for faith or for criticism; either to complete commitment or to open scepticism. An article in Nicolai's Berlin periodical, probably written by himself, mildly observed: 'There is room in the world for you and for us.'[5] This is precisely what Hamann denied. There is no room for truth and falsehood: one or the other must perish in the fight. The Jews must be kept in their place; so must all foreigners who bring disruptive ideas from the West. Yet he did not make common cause with the pamphleteers and clerical propagandists who attacked the Enlightenment. It is only after the death of Lessing that he allows himself to say that the notorious Pastor Goeze[6] may

---

[1] w iii 385.29 ff.   [2] w iii 193.37.   [3] w iii 194.1.

[4] w iii 410.5, w iv 462.6; cf. 1 Corinthians 1: 23: 'But we preach Christ crucified, unto the Jews a stumblingblock, and unto the Greeks foolishness.'

[5] *Allgemeine deutsche Bibliothek*, supplement to vols 25–36 (1775–8), part 4, p. 2479 (reprinted in *Hamann's Schriften*, vol. 8., ed. Gustav Adolph Weiner, part 1 (Berlin, 1842), p. 282).

[6] Lessing's most ferocious antagonist among the Lutheran clergy. An admirer of Lessing once said that he would rather be wrong with Lessing than right with Goeze.

in his own way have been right. Whatever his influence on later reactionaries, Hamann was too independent, too eccentric, too unruly a subject. of Frederick the Great to join in any man-hunt or collaborate in any government or Church campaign.

Far more typical of him is his defence of the letter *h*. In 1773 there appeared a volume entitled *Betrachtung über Religion* by C. T. Damm, an old Wolffian theologian much respected by the educated public of Berlin. Damm denounced the use of the letter *h* in many German words where it appeared to him to be superfluous, for instance between two syllables or after a consonant. Hamann published a riposte entitled *New Apology of the Letter H*.[1] This time he is no longer either Socrates or any of his more fearful impersonations – a crusading philosopher, a Rosicrucian knight on his death-bed, a sibyl, an apocalyptic mystagogue, Abelard Virbius, the Magus of the North,[2] the sage

---

[1] w iii 89–108.

[2] This description, which he liked himself, and by which he was known to many of his contemporaries and is referred to throughout discussion of him by writers in German in the last two centuries, was originally given him by F. K. von Moser. It is connected not merely with the fact that in 1762 he wrote a little essay on the Magi of the East at Bethlehem, in which as a special nail in Helvétius' coffin he says that what the Magi did was prima facie absurd – they deserted their kingdoms and subjects, mistook an old Eastern legend for good tidings, sought the cradle of a foreign child with deplorable consequences, allowed the Tetrarch Philip to massacre the innocents (a disastrous enterprise) – yet the implication of it (as of all genius) is that an 'outer' act may seem absurd to contemporaries, but if God is truly within, the deed is immortal and beyond price. It is due even more to the fact that Kepler had predicted that the planet Venus would pass the solar orbit in June 1761; in that year Captain Cook set off for the Southern Seas; the learned orientalist Michaelis persuaded Frederick V of Denmark to send a learned expedition to Arabia. Hamann sat down to the study of the Koran. Hence a concatenation of events which brought together the notion of the Magi, a star, an expedition to the East, in the slightly ironical, affectionate sobriquet 'Der Magus in Norden'.

Aristobulus, the angry prophet from the Brook Kerith, a Northern Savage, Zacchaeus the Publican, Ahasuerus Lazarus, Elijah *redivivus*, the Mandarin Mien Man Hoam, or a Protestant Minister in Swabia. Now he is masquerading as a simple old Prussian schoolmaster called Heinrich Schröder; he smokes his pipe, he drinks his mug of beer in the evening, he has three classes to attend to, and the letter *h*, the first letter of his Christian name, is dear to him.

What are Damm's arguments? That the unpronounced *h* is otiose, and, perhaps worse, may teach children blind faith, may rob them of critical powers. Language ought to be rationalised; it ought to be made sane, practical and free from all arbitrary elements. But this is impossible; a perfectly logical language is a chimera; all 'arbitrary' and non-logical elements cannot be taken out of life – that would leave it flat and dreary. The letter *h*, this parasitic letter, useless, a nuisance, embodies for Hamann the unpredictable element in reality, the element of fantasy in God's direction of the world. The tract grows into a diatribe against a spick and span, desiccated universe and a paean to irregularity and the beauty of the irrational. Leibniz's 'sufficient reason' is a lamentable, poor, blind, naked thing. 'Your life', says the letter *h*, addressing Damm and his ilk[1] – 'Your life is what I am myself, a breath [*ein Hauch*].'[2] God has created poor little useless *h*, but it will not perish from the earth. A tremendous and most moving hymn to God follows. Deists who prove God by design have no faith in such as me; such a God exists only by the precarious logic of vain,

---

[1] They are apostrophised as 'You little prophets of Böhmisch-Breda!', an allusion to *Le Petit Prophète de Boehmischbroda* (n.p., 1753), a pamphlet ostensibly reporting the vaticinations of a prophet born in a Bohemian village, actually by Baron Friedrich Melchior von Grimm, the celebrated Paris critic, a correspondent of Catherine the Great, a friend of Diderot, Holbach and many other figures of the Enlightenment.

[2] w iii 105.4.

puffed-up logicians – the logician is evidently logically prior to God. In such a universe I – *h* – could not survive, but thanks to the true God I do and shall.

It is no great distance from this to defending ancient institutions and usages as such for fear of killing the soul altogether with the body, as the French reformers seemed to Hamann on the way to doing. In a world built by Helvétius there would be no colour, no novelty, no genius, no thunder or lightning, no agony and no transfiguration. When the young Goethe spoke at Strasburg of how dark, how Cimmerian, how corpse-like Holbach's *System of Nature* appeared to him to be,[1] and spoke with rapture about the elemental, spontaneous poetry of Gothic cathedrals and the untamed German spirit, he supposed himself to be speaking under the influence of his new friend Herder; in fact both were echoing Hamann, who, in Germany at least, represents a solitary personal revolt against the entire embattled Enlightenment. He was a major force in transforming the ideas which hitherto had lived only in small, self-isolated religious communities, remote from and opposed to the great world, into weapons in the public arena. His was the first great shot in the battle of the romantic individualists against rationalism and totalitarianism.

---

[1] *Dichtung und Wahrheit*, book 11: p. 405 in Scheibe's edition (see p. 2 above, note 2).

6 LANGUAGE

HAMANN'S VIEW of language is at once the most central and the most original doctrine in the rich and disordered world of his ideas, and perhaps the most fertile: from the seed that he planted – as always and as if on principle, he did not tend the plant, but let it grow as it would – developed Herder's linguistic historicism and psychologism, and (nothing would have horrified Hamann more deeply) a powerful factor in modern linguistic analysis.

The middle of the eighteenth century witnessed a celebrated controversy, launched by Condillac in 1746,[1] about the origins of speech, dividing those who believed that it was of human invention from those who supposed that it must have been given to mankind by God. Those who thought speech a human creation claimed it was a product of either nature or art, which, by analogy with the development in other respects of the human organism, sprang initially from biological needs, and developed, as for instance Maupertuis had maintained in 1756,[2] from gestures and natural cries. Something of the sort – though with considerable differences – was expounded by De Brosses in 1765.[3] Other 'naturalist' theories were contained in James

---

[1] *Essai sur l'origine des connoissances humaines* (Amsterdam, 1746).

[2] 'Dissertation sur les différents moyens dont les hommes se sont servis pour exprimer leurs idées', a lecture delivered on 13 May 1756. *Oeuvres de Mr de Maupertuis* (Lyon, 1756), vol. 3, pp. 435–68.

[3] *Traité de la formation méchanique des langues et des principes physiques de l'étymologie* (Paris, 1765); translated into German as *De Brosse über Sprache und Schrift* (Leipzig, 1777).

Harris's *Hermes* (1751) and the famous treatise of Lord Mon-
boddo, *Of the Origin and Progress of Language* (1773–92).
Against this view arose an army of Christian theologians
led by J. P. Süssmilch,[1] who argued, as indeed Rousseau
had already claimed in his *Discours sur l'inégalité* of 1755,
that if language was a human invention, something that
man created to satisfy a need, it must have been a product
of thought, since reflection was an indispensable precon-
dition of language, just as language was of thought. But,
according to Süssmilch, all thought used symbols, and
therefore language, or at any rate symbolism, was presupposed in the act of inventing symbolism, which could not
therefore be a pure invention. This perfectly valid argument – valid, that is, against the bald notion that language
was a device created by man like the wheel or the screw –
became a commonplace of theological argument and is much
used by Bonald in his attempt at the refutation of Condillac.
For the consequence that Süssmilch and others drew from this
argument was that, since language is not a human creation,
it was communicated to man by God – it was a miraculous
gift of divine grace, like the human soul itself.

The greatest figure in this controversy was Herder, who
attacked Süssmilch with weapons drawn from Hamann himself. The notion of a complete language springing forth
fully armed, grammatical structure and all, before human
reason had developed to a relevant degree of sophistication,
is a chimera. All faculties grow; they are in a state of constant interplay (Hamann said '*jealousy*').[2] Language is one
of the expressions of this organic growing together and
mutual interpenetration of human faculties. It was neither

---

[1] Johann Peter Süssmilch, *Versuch eines Beweises, daß die erste Sprache
ihren Ursprung nicht vom Menschen, sondern allein vom Schöpfer erhalten habe*,
dating from 1756 but first published ten years later (Berlin, 1766).
One of Süssmilch's most eloquent and persuasive allies is Antoine Court
de Gébelin later in the century.

[2] w iii 237.28.

invented nor revealed as a fully shaped instrument that one fine day fell into the lap of an astonished and overjoyed man like a delightful, precious and unexpected gift. Like everything else it developed, *pari passu* with man's cognitive and emotional and other powers – *Kräfte* – in the course of time. No doubt, even though language was of human origin, 'it reveals *God in the light of a higher day*: his work is a human soul which itself creates and continues to create its own language because it is his work, because it is a human soul'.[1] It is no more and no less divine than any other human activity. God works within us immanently – man, and all he is and does, is made in his image, his from first to last.

Hamann had nothing against the anti-apriorism and anti-rationalism of this approach, but he was outraged by its – to him excessive – degree of naturalism: it endowed man with too much power, and nature with too much creative capacity. He attacked Herder bitterly, and Herder in due course recanted and came closer to Süssmilch's position and the notion that language and symbolism and thought were miraculously – or at any rate for no natural cause that is in principle discoverable – added to the attributes of the human animal, who was thus transformed into man, an immortal soul, a being in constant dialogue with his Lord, unlike anything else in nature. This controversy between two Protestant theologians – for in essence Hamann was that no less, indeed rather more, than Herder – stimulated Hamann to expound his theory of language, as always in fragments and sudden digressions, footnotes, irrelevant parentheses, but nevertheless with characteristic boldness and life.

Hamann's claim was in effect this: the notion that there is

---

[1] This was Herder's celebrated thesis in his work on the origin of language, *Abhandlung über den Ursprung der Sprache* (Berlin, 1772), at p. 221. See *Herders Sämmtliche Werke*, ed. Bernhard Suphan, vol. 5 (Berlin, 1891), p. 146. Hamann quotes the passage, with different emphases, at W iii 18.19.

a process called thought or reasoning that is an independent activity 'within' man, in some part of his brain or mind, which he can choose at will to articulate into a set of symbols which he invents for the purpose (or derives from others, fully formed), but which, alternatively, he can also conduct by means of unverbalised or unsymbolised ideas in some non-empirical medium, free from images, sounds, visual data, is a meaningless illusion – yet that is, of course, what men have often thought to be true, and indeed perhaps, for the most part, still think. Hamann is one of the first thinkers to be quite clear that thought *is* the use of symbols, that non-symbolic thought, that is, thought without either symbols or images – whether visual or auditory, or perhaps a shadowy combination of the two, or perhaps derived from some other sense, kinaesthetic or olfactory (though this is less likely in man as we know him) – is an unintelligible notion.[1] To think, in all the many senses of that concept, is to employ something – images, marks on paper, sounds – intentionally, that is, to denote objects: things, persons, events, facts. What symbols are used to do the denoting is another question: some may be traced to unconscious roots and biological and physiological causes, others to artificial invention, as of new words, technical terminology and the like. But in all cases thought (or language) is the employment of symbols. Vico had said something very close to this, but Hamann – like the rest of the learned world, apart from a few Italian savants – had evidently not read him.[2]

---

[1] There is a story that the economist J. M. Keynes, when asked whether he thought in words or images, replied, 'I think in thoughts.' This is amusing but, if Hamann is right, absurd.

[2] He did order a copy of the *Scienza nuova* in 1777, and was disappointed when he received it, for he had assumed from its title that it dealt with the subject of political economy, which interested him; in any case, he formulated his own theory well before this; if there were Vichian influences via Italian Homeric scholars who were read in Germany, there is no evidence that the *New Science* directly influenced Hamann.

'Language is the first and last organ and criterion of reason,' said Hamann.[1] The Cartesian notion that there are ideas, clear and distinct, which can be contemplated by a kind of inner eye, a notion common to all the rationalists, and peddled in its empirical form by Locke and his followers – ideas in their pure state, unconnected with words and capable of being translated into any of them indifferently – this is the central fallacy that for him needed eliminating. The facts were otherwise. Language is what we think with, not translate into: the meaning of the notion of 'language' is symbol-using. Images came before words,[2] and images are created by passions.[3] Our images, and later our words (which are but images used in a systematic fashion according to rules, although Hamann, with his hatred of system, scarcely concedes even this; he would like to feel that language is a spontaneous outpouring, a kind of gesturing that others understand directly), are coloured, altered by the least change in our sense-experience. Our art and thought and religion spring from the same root, our response to outside factors, in Hamann's case God, who speaks to us like a father and teaches us the rudiments of language, and thereby articulates our world for us; as our symbols go, so go our concepts and categories, which are but arrangements of symbols. This, if it is translated into non-theistic language, can be represented as a response to nature and to other human beings. Indeed, Hamann adds the latter: man thinks and acts in response to others like himself; his nature is not intelligible save in terms of perpetual communication – with God and with other beings – and by means of reminiscence of his own past self,[4] a reminiscence of something taught to him by God, or, as empiricists would say, by other human beings, his parents or teachers.

---

[1] w iii 284.24.   [2] w ii 199.4 ff.   [3] w ii 208.20, 25.
[4] Language, like all learning, 'is not mere *invention*, but rather a *reminiscence*' (w iii 41.11).

All speech, all art, all reflection, are reducible to different uses of symbolism. Hamann's new aesthetics – here too he showed originality of a high order – is founded on the proposition that the language and the form of art are indissolubly one with the art itself, as against the dominant aesthetic theorists – Boileau or Batteux or Gottsched and their disciples – who maintained that rules existed for the purpose of rendering an identical 'content' into the best or most appropriate 'vehicle' or medium, and so distinguished content, form, style, language, as independent and manipulable constituents of a compound substance – something that for Hamann was one indissoluble 'organic' entity. Sometimes he says of sense and reason that they are like angels moving up and down Jacob's Ladder, intermingling, in the end homogeneous and not sharply distinguishable.[1]

What is it to understand? If you wish to understand the Bible you must comprehend 'the Oriental character of the eloquence of the flesh that takes us to the cradle of our race and our religion'.[2] 'Every court, every school, every profession, every closed corporation, every sect – each has its own vocabulary.'[3] How do we penetrate this? With the passion of 'a friend, an intimate, a lover'[4] – faith and belief are the motifs again – above all, not by rules. The same applies even to theology. He was much excited by Luther's remark, which he found in Bengel, that theology was nothing but grammar concerned with the words of the Holy Ghost.[5] For what is theology but the study of the actual words of God spoken to us? Words – not ideas or truths which might have been articulated in some other fashion and symbolism, yet have borne literally the same sense: for sense and words are one, and all translation distorts. Some

---

[1] e.g. w iii 287.29.   [2] w ii 170.37.   [3] w ii 172.21.
[4] w ii 171.15.
[5] Johann Albrecht Bengel, *Gnomon novi testamenti in quo ex nativa verborum vi simplicitas, profunditas, concinnitas, salubritas sensuum coelestium indicatur* (Tübingen, 1742), preface, section 14, p. [xxiv]. See B ii 10.1 ff.

sentences may resemble one another, or carry similar meanings, but no sentence can literally be substituted for any other, for the connection of words and sense is organic, indissoluble, unique. Words are the living carriers of feeling – only pedants and scholars dilute them by analysis or kill them with devitalising formulae. A word is the stamp of life – the richer the better.

Goethe and Jacobi are witnesses to the magnetic force of Hamann's cryptic style – something that he deliberately adopted, half regretting his own obscurity, half accepting it as an antidote to abstraction, as the only way to attempt to convey the fullness of the inexhaustible particulars of which the world was composed. He was intent upon creating a sense of unplumbed depths, of unlimited vistas, and stopping efforts to define, delimit, close in tidy formulae; he applauds irregularity, luxuriance, the inexhaustible and indescribable, the astonishing, the miraculous, the strokes of lightning, the sudden momentary illumination of the dark. He spoke in riddles, but those who admired him were fascinated by this mysterious, deep man and the unusual, startling perspectives that he seemed to open. No man was ever in more conscious opposition to his age, with a fanaticism that often turned into blind perversity. 'For me', he said, 'every book is a Bible.'[1] And by this he certainly wished to imply no kind of pantheism, which he would have regarded as a shallow heresy. What he meant was that every author animates his book, that it is his living expression, that to understand it one needs direct insight, a sense of the author, his time, his intentions, the world that he inhabits, the vision of which his expression is a part, and this is needed above all to attain to even the most fleeting glimpse, the most insufficient knowledge, of what God said to us in his book, or in his nature, his history. It is this contrast between the sense of dialogue, communication,

[1] B i 309.11.

immediate understanding, achieved by what Herder was to call 'feeling into' (*Einfühlung*) a man, or a style or a period, with rational, rule-dominated analysis that to some extent Goethe may have derived from Hamann.

Whenever he embarks on amateur philological excursions of his own, what he seeks is the essence of the meaning of a word, a work of art, a ritual, a way of life, not an exotic vision into which to escape from the real world. For example, his suggestion that all mythological rivers are masculine, because not *flumen* but *vir* or *amnis* is the suppressed subject in their titles, shows a Vico-like desire to comprehend some inner process, a vision of the world on the part of men remote in time and space; it does not reflect a yearning to return to the Middle Ages, like that German linguistic nationalism which Swiss scholars such as Bodmer and Breitinger, or even the liberal Gottsched, displayed, but which to Hamann appears to be an unworthy unrealism and a rejection of the real world in favour of some historical fiction. It is with this attitude that he infected his disciple Herder, when he urged him to study the poetry of the Letts, which, he suggested, may have had something to do with the rhythm of their work,[1] or drew his attention to a learned work on Icelandic sagas. Language and thought are one, like God and his Shekinah and Tabernacle.[2] 'Where there is no word there is no reason – and no world.'[3] 'All idle talk about reason is mere wind; language is its organon and criterion!'[4] That is why Kant, who supposes himself to be speaking about the categories and concepts of something that he calls the understanding, is in fact speaking about forms of language – a fluid, mercury-like substance that alters not only with entire forms of life but with individuals, with attitudes, with professions, with moods. To suppose

---

[1] An idea which crops up in Henri de Saint-Simon and Marx, but not, so far as I know, in Herder.
[2] W iii 237.10.   [3] B v 95.21.   [4] B v 108.6.

that one is laying down, once and for all, the eternal, unalterable laws of something called thought, translatable into any language and any symbolism – some inner, rock-like reality, of which language is merely the cover or the glove, made to fit, an artificial thing – that is the profoundest misunderstanding of all.

There is no non-symbolic thought or knowledge. All thinkers who have believed that actual forms of language conveyed error, which could be detected by non-verbal means, and that a new language could be invented to convey the truth more exactly – who did not, in other words, use language as an instrument of self-criticism, but tried to get in some sense behind it (as, for instance, Leibniz and such modern philosophers as even the verbally sensitive Russell have sometimes supposed themselves to be doing) – appear to Hamann to be engaged upon a nonsensical undertaking, something that ignores the essence of the situation. For him, as for Berkeley, the world is God's language; that is, just as we think in symbols, God thinks in trees or battles, or rocks and seas, as well as in the Hebrew and Greek letters of his inspired prophets, who spoke not in their own name but in his. This vision never leaves him:

> Every phenomenon of nature was a name – the sign, the symbol, the promise of a fresh and secret and ineffable but all the more intimate chosen union, communication and communion of divine energies and ideas. All that man in these beginnings heard with his ears, saw with his eyes, contemplated or touched with his hands, all this was the living word. For God was the Word. With the Word in his mouth and in his heart, the origin of language was as natural, as near and as easy as a child's play.[1]

This is how it was with Adam in Paradise, but then there was the Fall, arrogance, the Tower of Babel, an attempt to

[1] w iii 32.21.

substitute for the immediacy of sense and direct perception cold constructions of theoretical reason.

For Hamann thought and language are one (even though he sometimes contradicts himself and speaks as if there could be some kind of translation from one to the other).[1] Because this is so, philosophy, which pretends to be the critique of things, or at best ideas about them, since it is nothing but words about words – second-order judgements – is in fact a critique of our use of language or symbols. If it had been the case that there was a metaphysical structure of things which could somehow be directly perceived, or if there were a guarantee that our ideas, or even our linguistic usage, in some mysterious way corresponded to such an objective structure, it might be supposed that philosophy, either by direct metaphysical intuition, or by attending to ideas or to language, and through them (because they correspond) to the facts, was a method of knowing and judging reality. But for Hamann this is a thoroughly fallacious conception, though time-honoured – indeed one on which the whole of European rationalism has been built. The notion of a correspondence, that there is an objective world on one side, and, on the other, man and his instruments – language, ideas and so forth – attempting to approximate to this objective reality, is a false picture. There is only a flow of sensations, inner and outer, colours, tastes, sights, sounds, smells, love and hatred, sorrow, pity, indignation, awe, worship, hope, remorse, rage, conflict; and above all faith, hope, love, directed towards persons – other human beings or the Creator and the Father of the world and of men, Almighty God.

We become conscious of this flow of experience – beyond which there are only nature and history, by which God speaks to us. Our acceptance of these realities is founded on faith – or Hume's belief. We learn through the medium

[1] e.g. 'To speak is to translate', w ii 199.4.

of symbolism, and our creative imagination conceives the past and the future that are absent, or the possibilities that are not yet and perhaps never will be, or what might have happened but did not, through the medium of the selfsame symbols. But the essence of symbolism is communication: communication between me and others or me and God, which is of the essence of being human at all. That, of course, is one of the reasons why it is absurd to suppose that human society is founded, or should be founded, on a promise or desire for utility or avoidance of danger or some other 'rational' consideration – that it was constructed by such calculation or can be justified in terms of it, so that if the justification were successfully refuted, we could, and rationally should, dissolve society and live in some other way. The truth is, of course, for Hamann, that man comes to recognise himself to be what he is only in the context of the relationships of which in a sense he is compounded, in the first place relationships to God, to other persons and to nature, in the second his own constructs out of these relationships – institutions, sciences, arts, forms of life, hopes and ideals. Above all, of course, this network of relationships is held together by the pervasiveness of the paternity and constant tutelage of God.

The image is, as it were, of an entity – man – engaged in perpetual activity, or construction of his own and others' lives, with bricks provided by sensation and imagination, called symbols, which are sometimes mistakenly denominated abstract notions, thought of as having an independent life of their own; sometimes still more mistakenly (as by medieval philosophical realists) viewed as non-sensuous, eternal characteristics of a transcendent world, called universals – eternal, unchangeable denizens of a supernatural world, which Plato conceived in one way and Descartes in another, and Kant (although Hamann misrepresents him gravely in this respect) in yet another. But in fact all there is is a world of persons, and their ways of conceiving their own experience – ways determined by the apparatus that determines their relationships. This is what he means by saying that creation is speech[1] or 'through [language] are *all things* made',[2] or when he describes human speech as a form of creative energy. That is why the cardinal sin is 'to confuse *words* with *concepts* and *concepts* with *real things*',[3] which is precisely what metaphysicians have done, hemming man in with imaginary entities of his own construction, which he then proceeds to worship as if they were real forces or divinities, and which distort his life (this is a vast and pregnant generalisation of Rousseau's and Diderot's notion of human alienation) because of the conflict between what man truly is – self-expressive, creative, loving (or hating) – and the standards that he has invented (without intending to), social, moral, aesthetic, philosophical, in terms of an imaginary being. This being, whose favour he seeks, to whom he seeks to approximate, to whom he wishes to justify himself, is a monstrosity of his own creation which he has set up in judgement over himself and calls 'public opinion' or 'the common morality of mankind' or 'the State' or 'the Church', or conceives as some more personal, and if anything more despotic, divinity, before which he quakes, whose authority he accepts as absolute, but which, on examination, turns out to be a figment, an obsession, due to some weakness or blunder, some blindness to reality, and the attempt to make up for this by a grotesque invention of man's perverted intellect or imagination.

Diderot, in the famous 'Paradox of the Comedian',[4] spoke of the contrast between natural action and assuming a role: 'The man of sensibility obeys only the impulses of nature, and utters nothing but a cry from his heart; as soon as he tries to moderate or force this cry it is no longer he, it is

---

[1] B i 393.28.   [2] B vi 108.24.   [3] B v 264.36.

[4] *Paradoxe sur le comédien* (published posthumously in 1830). See F. C. Green (ed.), *Diderot's Writings on the Theatre* (Cambridge, 1936), pp. 249–317.

a comedian who is playing.'[1] And again: 'One is oneself by
nature; one is another by imitation.'[2] This 'otherness', this
acting of a role imposed upon one, imposed perhaps by the
unintended consequences of the behaviour of one's self or
one's fellows in the past, which comes to threaten and coerce
one as if it were a real entity menacing one from outside –
that is the phenomenon of alienation, to which Rousseau
and Hegel, Kierkegaard and Marx, and much modern psychology and sociology have given a central role.

Hamann, although he does not call it by that name, is
among those who originated this approach to man's condition. For him, as indeed for many a Christian thinker,
man is alienated, a being who is estranged from the source
of reality – God and other men, and the immediacy of
feeling and sense-experience. As soon as man starts to construct another world, to redress the balance of something
that he has lost in this one – the abstract world of the
sciences, the super-sensible world of metaphysics – he is
done for. This is metaphysics, illusion, idolatry, self-
frustration, of the most fatal kind. This is at the root of
Hamann's new notion of language.

There are many stages in the fall from grace. First there
is the effort on the part of the Enlightenment to cut reason
off from custom and tradition and all faith in them.[3] This
is called the autonomy of reason. Then there is an attempt
to cut man off from his own individual experience and
establish universal laws for all men as such, at any time and
any place, as made, for instance, by Descartes or Kant. The
worst of all is the divorce from words, the effort to suggest
that one can grasp meanings in a naked, wordless state; but
this always fails, for without words there is no thinking,
and words are not timeless uniform entities, but change
with every individual and social and historical tremor. He
speaks of words, but to extend this to all symbols – anything

[1] ibid., p. 277. [2] ibid., p. 296. [3] w iii 284.8.

intended to communicate – does not alter his meaning. Anyone who professes to be able to talk about pure form independently of its matter cheats in this way – that is what Kant is accused of with his '*gnostic* hatred of matter' and '*mystical* love of form'.[1] Kant speaks of paralogisms – the paradoxes of rationality – but they come not through the misuse of reason, whatever that may mean, but through the misuse of language, through not understanding how language functions in our perception and interpretation of reality, above all in our action, which is at one with our thought and feeling. This is a very modern doctrine, and when Hamann says to Herder, in one of the most profoundly felt of his tormented, seemingly endless pieces of self-examination, 'Reason is language, *logos*. On this marrow-bone I gnaw, and shall gnaw myself to death on it',[2] he stakes out one of his greatest claims to immortality. It was a just summary of what preoccupied him all his life, and he had not long to live when he said it.

To be conscious – to discriminate – is to use symbols. Symbols or words are not invented by their user, but are given him as a free gift by divine grace, by the 'great all-giver'.[3] To understand or think is to participate in the drama that is the creation.[4] We are free to take part in the drama or to resign from it and perish – determinism is a scientific fiction. But we are not free to be what we wish, for we are created to be and do what we are and do. Herder is sharply criticised for supposing that language is a natural function, that it grows like the sense of smell or taste – for Hamann everything is a gift from a personal deity. Herder, after recanting, nevertheless leapt back into his naturalism towards the end of his life and attempted to give an empirical-genetic explanation of how different languages developed and what relations they had to the geographical,

---

[1] w iii 285.15.   [2] B v 177.18.   [3] w iii 38.3.
[4] cf. B iii 104.26.

biological, and psychological and social characteristics of their users. Hamann thinks that there is an organic connection between all these attributes, and that history may indeed reveal it, but what is important for him is to insist that the connection created by God and history itself is only a kind of enormous living allegory. The facts, of course, occur as they do and the events that historians uncover did indeed occur, and it is possible to re-establish them by painstaking scholarship; but his point is that we can read in these patterns of events and facts what man is, what his purposes are, what God has created him for; and we can read this in the Bible also; we can read this in the economy of nature; and for Hamann that is all that is of importance.

It may be that others are interested in the facts for their own sake, to satisfy their curiosity; and invent or study sciences in order to satisfy this same curiosity; or perhaps they do so the better to control material forces. All this may be so, but to him this seems trivial beside the need to answer the ultimate questions: Why are we here? What are we at? What are our goals? How can we allay the spiritual agony of those who will not rest unless they obtain true answers to these questions? Nature is like the Hebrew alphabet. It contains only consonants. The vowels we must supply for ourselves, otherwise we cannot read the words.[1] How do we supply them? By that faith – or belief – of which Hume had spoken, without which we could not live for an instant; by our unbreakable certainty that there exists an external world, that there exists God, that there exist other human beings with whom we are in communication – this is presupposed by all other knowledge. To suppose it to be false, to doubt it, is nothing but self-refuting scepticism, the denial of that consciousness without which we could not even have formulated the doubt. *Cogito ergo est.*

Man begins with sensations and images and therefore

---

[1] B i 450.19.

with song and poetry, which precede prose[1] as forms of
spontaneous self-expression – not under the pressure of
solely material needs. Whereas Herder was inclined at times
towards a historical materialism in his history of civilisation,
Hamann will have none of this. 'As gardens come before
the cultivation of fields, painting before writing, singing
before speech, metaphors before reasoning, barter before
trade',[2] so luxuries may come before necessities. Necessity
is not the mother of invention, else why should orientals
be the first to clothe themselves, while Red Indians shiver?[3]
Rather than trace contemporary reason to primitive beginnings he prefers to note the signs of the survival of primitive
unreason in modern life. Why should we assume that primi-
tives are unthinking, semi-animal creatures whose whole
life is exhausted in struggle, survival – in action? Although
'their movement was a tumultuous dance', yet they 'sat for
seven days in silent meditation or amazement and opened
their lips for wingèd words'.[4] In other words, in every stage
of life, even the earliest, there is God, wonder, revelation,
meditation, not just corporeal needs.

There is no evidence that Hamann knew anything about
primitive man; such passages are pure imagination. Their
value is only in illustrating his ever-present fear that the
fullness of human life and the many-sidedness of human
character may be misrepresented, narrowed, done injustice
to, by being squeezed into the framework of some a priori
scientific schema conceived by some fanatical arranger of
facts. To understand the past we must in the first place
understand the words used by those who made it. Scholars

---

[1] Vico had said this before, but, as I have mentioned, nobody in
the eighteenth century save perhaps a few scholars in Naples had paid
attention to his work. The English scholars Bishop Lowth – in his
Lectures on the Sacred Poetry of the Hebrews – and Blackwell, who said
something of this sort, did not perceive its implications, and Voltaire,
who reviewed Lowth in 1766, did not see them either.

[2] W ii 197.15.   [3] W ii 198.17 ff.   [4] W ii 197.18.

87

are often least gifted in this respect. The great orientalist
J. D. Michaelis of Göttingen, in his book *The Dead Tongue
of the Hebrews*, provides a characteristic example of 'philosophical myopia'.[1] The language of the Hebrews is not dead,
only its treatment by Professor Michaelis is so. There is not
a trace in his great work of any acquaintance with the spirit
of the men who wrote in this language, because he has
repressed within himself the sensuous element and allowed
the intellectual, reasoning faculty too much play; this pro-
duces a mountain of useless scholarship. How is this to
be remedied? Only by abandoning the smooth Aristotelian
methods of the eighteenth century, in which man is conceived as peacefully developing towards his appointed end –
his preconceived purpose – in a rational, harmonious,
inexorable way. We must delve into the depths and splendours of the ravaged human soul. The eighteenth century
is not even blasphemous, simply blind to the abyss, and
therefore blind to the grandeur of its creator. For this the
pagan Goethe duly praises him, and so perhaps might Freud
have done, who was no Christian either, and for the very
same reason. Society is founded on language.[2] 'The history
of a people is in its language.'[3] As the life of the people,
so its language and its dialects. The relations of symbols
are to Hamann not unlike the relations between persons.[4]
There is no universal reason any more than a universal
language – a 'natural language' is as absurd as 'natural
religion', 'natural law' and all the other fictions of the metaphysicians. Everything is concrete, is and was where it is
in the world, in its specific relations to other concrete entities, and cannot be grasped without some faculty other
than the generalising faculty that analyses everything into
uniform units, and then wonders where the variety, the
colour, the meaning have gone. The German romantic

[1] W ii 123.12.   [2] W iii 300.31.   [3] B i 393.23.
[4] B v 40.16, 51.28.

school of philosophy was destined to make much of these polemical claims.

Hamann spoke out of a considerable knowledge of languages. He knew French and English, Latin and Greek, Italian, Portuguese and some Lettish as well as Hebrew and a certain amount of Arabic; he denounced translation, which loses precisely what distinguishes one type of inner experience from another; and he believed that a man can truly create only in his own native language. 'Who writes in his native tongue has the rights of the father of a family', and can fulfil his whole nature 'if he has the power to exercise these rights', whereas 'he who writes in a foreign tongue has to bend his spirit to it like a lover'.[1] A man, to create properly, must be master of his words, so that he can even misuse them if he will. Those who follow the rules of academies or the good taste of their society are like hired rhymesters who follow slavishly the thoughts of others. Authenticity is all. To be the servant of a master is ultimate degradation, even when the master is some impersonal authority, that is, not human, but official or imaginary (this again echoes Rousseau, whom on other grounds he thought much too abstract). Hence his objection to reform, whether of language or anything else – it seems to him a wilful revolt against God's order, in which alone we can harmoniously fulfil ourselves, or at least suffer those conflicts from the torment of which we shall emerge purified and strengthened. Hence his criticism of F. G. Klopstock[2] (whose sincere religious faith, patriotism and ecstatic flights he truly admired) for wishing to introduce syntactical reforms; all this emerges in an ironical form in *New Apology of the Letter H*, already referred to. It is all part and parcel of Hamann's passionate conviction that man is one, and his life is one;

---

[1] w ii 126.9.

[2] The famous and very pious German poet, author of the Christian epic *Messias*, about which Herder, the head of the Lutheran Church in Weimar, complained that it was not German enough!

that letter is spirit, and spirit is letter; that letter without spirit is not even a letter; while spirit without letter does not exist at all.

He believes for this reason that private life cannot be sharply divided from public. Hence a State without a Church is a lifeless corpse, 'carrion for eagles',[1] while a Church without a State is a ghost, a scarecrow to frighten birds, and Mendelssohn and his rationalist friends, who wished to found a State on the need for security and public peace, were nothing but the reincarnation of the atheistical Hobbes – a man who wished to cut into the living flesh of society and turn it into a utilitarian device. This Hamann declares to be death and nausea – the turning of life into a mechanism, the killing of everything by which men live.[2] It was almost certainly he who inspired Herder with his interest in oriental literature and the Graeco-Roman classics, in popular speech, and in the intimate connections between language, thought, environment, and the physiological structure of different human types. This set Herder off on the road that led him to the creation of social psychology, of the view of men as deeply rooted in a texture of beliefs, institutions, forms of life, in terms of which alone they can be accounted for and their thought and action explained; to the creation of a new aesthetics of art as the sensual expression of individual or collective personality, a form of moral social commitment, as against earlier theories of art as embellishment or imitation or instruction or inspired utterance detached from daily life. In spite of this Herder went his own way, and attempted to use the findings of the natural sciences of his day to explain the evolution of human society; while Hamann rejected the great advances in the midst of which he lived as abstract schemas – counter-

---

[1] W iii 303.13.
[2] *Golgotha und Scheblimini!* (W iii 291–320), an attack on Mendelssohn's political tract, is entirely concerned with this theme.

feit goods, 'false noses',[1] 'empty sacks'[2] – and while passionately defending empiricism and glorifying Hume – an enemy who could not help speaking the truth – as against Kant, united it with a kind of mystical nominalism and belief in divine inspiration. As we cannot eat an egg without the faith for which no reason can in principle be given, so we know that God has spoken to us, and no one can argue us out of this, for all argument presupposes the faculty that guarantees the truth of divine revelation; and since one can understand only if one enters into the body and spirit of a symbolism which is the articulate expression of the soul, one must study and restudy the words of Holy Writ with which God created our world for us, and told us what to be, and revealed to us – as happened one night in London when Hamann saw his own life written large in the chronicles of the ancient Hebrews – what we are made of, what we must hope and fear and do.

Unger says that Hamann was both sensual and pious, and that in this way he was able to unite these two characteristics in a single doctrine. But the situation is odder than this. There is a union in Hamann's writings, not merely of sensual appetite and simple pietism, but of, on the one hand, a new and original theory of language and its relation to reality that was destined to celebrate its greatest triumphs in our own time, and, on the other, devout, passionate, uncritical absorption in every syllable of Holy Writ, and a polemic against the pretensions of reason far more vehement and far-reaching – and baseless – than that which Kant represented himself as attempting to achieve in order to make room for faith.[3] Kant's account of this faith is shadowy: Hamann's is passionate, vivid and concrete through and through. As a defender of the concrete, the particular, the intuitive, the personal, the unsystematic – this is the

---

[1] B vii 460.27.   [2] B vii 172.33.
[3] See further the Appendix on p. 129.

tendency which, for such cultural historians as Troeltsch and Meinecke, distinguishes, indeed divides, the Germans from the rational, generalising, scientific West – he has no equal. He is a true forerunner of Schelling, of Nietzsche and of the existentialists, and a dangerous ally of any supporter of organised religion.

7   CREATIVE GENIUS

IN MOST histories of German and European literature Hamann – if he is mentioned at all – is considered as one of the inspirers of the German literary movement known as the *Sturm und Drang*, among the most prominent attributes of which were a belief in self-abandonment to spontaneous feeling and passion, hatred of rules, and a desire for unbridled self-expression and self-assertion on the part of the artist, whether in life or in the creation of his works – the conception of the poet, the thinker, as a superior being, subject to agonies not known to the common run of men, seeking to realise himself in some unique, violent, unheard-of fashion, obedient to his own passion and will alone. This is in part true. Hamann, who mildly scandalised his contemporaries by placing the emblem of a hornèd Pan on some of his works, by his writings probably helped to stimulate some of his contemporaries into violent outbreaks against classicism and order, and did emphasise the irrational sources of man's creative power. If he did not encourage divine frenzy, he had less against it than the champions of neo-classicism among whom he lived.

Nevertheless his romanticism needs a good deal of qualification. He was not a 'heaven-storming' irrationalist. When J. K. Lavater wrote to him confessing to spiritual agonies because he was not sure of his faith, Hamann replied: 'Eat your bread joyfully, drink your wine with good heart – for your work pleases God.'[1] To be concerned too deeply about

---

[1] B iv 5.17.

one's own spiritual condition is to lack faith in God, that simple childlike faith upon which all rests; self-doubts and self-tortures (although Hamann was not a stranger to them) are mere pathological symptoms. To Jacobi, who complained that he could not reconcile his head and his heart, he replied in similar terms – submission, not Promethean struggle, is the way to serenity and truth, however great the obstacles in our path. Our parents heard 'the voice of God walking in the garden in the cool of the evening'.[1] We may never be able to return to this, but that is the radiant vision in the light of which we must live. We are all God's children – so long as we live in this knowledge, we shall not go astray.

So, too, he told the Roman Catholic Princess Golitsyn, who was troubled by her unquiet conscience, about whether she had done all that it was right for a good Christian to have done, and lived a sufficiently pure and dedicated life, that she should sow her seed and trust in God. Do not wait for the seed to bloom; do not look for a quiet conscience too anxiously – one must learn to support one's 'nothingness' (*Nichtigkeit*) and have faith in God's mercy. One must do what appears right to oneself and then let well alone. To be preoccupied with one's virtue is appalling arrogance and a wall against God. She was particularly troubled about the education of her children. From her journal we learn that Hamann's tranquil sermon on the holiness of humility, on the need to learn to be contented, indeed happy, in one's own insignificance, liberated her from her self-torment. God speaks to us through his works, through the world that he gave us, and in particular to our senses – do not seek to reduce him or his world to some inner core, some irreducible and ultimate entity. Accept what is given – flesh, passions – and do not attempt to explain them, transform them, or

[1] w iii 31.30, alluding to Genesis 3: 8.

deduce them. What is given is given; to learn to submit is to learn to understand.

Nevertheless Hamann naturally has thoughts about genius that are of interest. The notion of the free, spontaneous, creative impulse in man that knows no rules, or creates as the wind blows – this penetrates, as might be expected, everything that he wrote; he was not, of course, its originator, but he gave it a new and historically important direction. The notion that genius is a divine afflatus, so that the artist himself does not always know what it is that he is making, since he is but an instrument through which a higher – superhuman – power is speaking, is at least as old as Plato's *Ion*. Young's celebrated essay on the subject[1] released a great volume of pent-up German feeling on this topic. The second half of the eighteenth century is full of denunciations of narrowness and specialisation – of anything that cribs and confines men and prevents the richest realisation of the 'complete man', which is conceived as a harmonious process, prevented hitherto only by human error or vice and the destructive institutions that this has bred. This is not confined to German writers: Diderot, too, speaks of the battle between the natural and the artificial man within civilised man, and Rousseau's sermon on the destructive effect of man's institutions upon those who are brought up under them is well enough known. But the real revolt against neo-classicism is German, and directed against the ascendancy of the thinkers of Paris.

Although Hamann was among the earliest European thinkers to protest against the effect of French education and French doctrines based on a false psychology and a false view of God and of nature, this is not where his strongest claim to originality in this field lies. He is not principally interested in creating conditions in which a small group of the elect may be able to express themselves freely at the

[1] *Conjectures on Original Composition* (1759).

expense of, or at any rate beyond the horizon of, the common man. Nor is he interested in the social conception of genius as it was treated, for instance, by the French Encyclopaedists, some of whom thought that in a rationally organised society any man could in principle be transformed into a genius, as for example Trotsky seemed to believe (this is what Diderot, with his customary sense of reality, mocked so exquisitely in his essay on Helvétius' *On Man*); nor is he with Mendelssohn and Nicolai, who conceived of genius as consisting in the communication of ideas until they became universally accepted and so raised human life to a new level.

As against the stress on social conditions, Hamann believed that genius was individual and incapable of being bred or cultivated by social organisation; each man was as he was, saw what he saw, and spoke to those who understood him – not everyone, but those with whom he had special rapport; how large or small a number, there was no telling. Against Mendelssohn and Nicolai he maintained that only the free can understand or inspire or be inspired; and freedom consists in being at once one's master and one's most faithful subject; acceptance of general rules was always slavery – 'he who trusts the judgement of another more than his own ceases to be a man'.[1] Even though Winckelmann had said that by imitating the Greeks modern man would become inimitable, Hamann remained suspicious. Like Prometheus, we must steal the divine fire, not make a picture of it: he who wishes to rob the arts of fantasy and arbitrary freedom is making an attempt on their honour and their life. We must commit 'a Promethean plagiarism of the primal, animal light of nature';[2] hence the dichotomy of originality and slavery, spontaneity and abdication; hence, also, the hostility to classical models and utilitarian or other brands of moral and aesthetic didacticism.

[1] B i 377.35. [2] w iii 22.16.

But this is not Hamann's principal concern. He is not interested in the needs of the artistic élite. He is a moralist and a critic of life, and wishes to go to war with the enemies of mankind in general; he wishes to help to liberate human beings as such. His originality consists in translating the appeal to the authority of the individual conscience and the rejection of institutional authority, which came to him from his pietist upbringing, to the whole of life; save that by a self he means something that is in constant communication with others and with God, and sees the truth, practical and theoretical, only through the medium of these relationships and submission to them – self-knowledge (which for him is obtained in communion with God) is not a threat against one's freedom, not a painful act of artificial self-discipline. He rejects with both hands the puritanism of the pietists: the notion that man is no more than an unclean vessel, a mass of sin and corruption, and that since all men are accursed they must seek to root out of themselves all natural desires: 'Victory consists in death; life in dying', as a line of contemporary pietist verse runs.[1]

Hamann is as passionately opposed to this as he is to the utilitarian harmonisation of the passions, as advocated by the French *philosophes*. He goes so far as to accept the pietists' doctrine that reason is a poisonous snake, the arch-heretic, the great enemy of God and his truth – thus Johann Konrad Dippel,[2] who, like Schopenhauer after him, thought that all suffering was caused by a thirst that could never be satisfied, and tried to demonstrate this by instances of children who died ecstatically. But thereafter Hamann parts

---

[1] *Nordische Sammlungen, welche unterschiedene Exempel einer lebendigen und wahren Gottseligkeit, im Reiche Schweden, in sich halten . . .*, vol. [1] ([Altona], 1755), part 1, p. 123. (Copy in Royal Library, Stockholm.)

[2] *Christen-Statt auff Erden ohne gewöhnlichen Lehr-, Wehr- und Nehr-Stand . . .* (n.p., 1700; published under the pseudonym 'Christianus Democritus'), pp. 18, 78–9, 111. (Microfilm in Taylor Institution Library, Oxford.)

company with this grim sect far more sharply than does their other scion, Immanuel Kant. His words of praise for his peasant common-law wife[1] – indeed, his motive for living with her – are rooted in his love of what seemed to him healthy, innocent, natural, free from the self-torture to which the misuse of our God-given sense and languages leads the learned: better provincialism, roots in local life, than bloodless uniformity, hot-house plants, the death in life of sophisticated academics; the greatest crime is to divorce the intellect from 'the deepest abysses of the most tangible sensuousness'.[2] 'Let there be light!'[3] This is joy in creation, sensuous joy. God himself was made flesh, else he could not discourse to us, who also are flesh; but we have divided the spirit and the flesh. 'To gather the fragments together – *disjecti membra poetae* – is the work of a scholar; to interpret them, of a philosopher; to imitate them or shape them [*sie in Geschick bringen*], of the poet.'[4] Poetry gives unity and life. So, too, history is only a valley of dead bones,[5] unless a prophet comes, like Ezekiel, to clothe them with flesh.

To live truly and to create is one: this is the gist of the 'rhapsody in cabbalistic prose' hurled at Michaelis' head in 1762 under the title of 'Aesthetics in a Nutshell'.[6] 'Leben ist *actio*'[7] – life is action, not some impersonal metaphysical power, the self-developing Idea of Hegel, or the *praxis* of Marx, which it is difficult to identify in concrete spatial or temporal terms, something which even in the most materialistic terminology retains the mythical quality of its metaphysical origins; but day-to-day action, faith in instinct, in that understanding without which there is no communication with others, in direct face-to-face encounters with

---

[1] B iii 262.21.   [2] w iii 287.31.   [3] w ii 197.26.
[4] w ii 198.34.   [5] w ii 176.12.
[6] *Aesthetica in nuce* (w ii 195–217): 'A Rhapsody in Cabbalistic Prose' is Hamann's subtitle.
[7] B iv 288.29.

things or men, in the fullness of life. This is how artists create, but it is also how all men achieve the realisation of what is most human in them, how societies achieve unity of spirit, their members that blend of practical wisdom and love and sensuous satisfaction that distinguishes full human beings from the absurd two-dimensional figments of theorists, and from that inner desiccation and alienation in the theorists themselves which cause them to confound real life with their bloodless, stylised categories. A connoisseur who sits in his study, contemplating now a picture upon his wall, now a volume upon his table, is not a living human being at all, but a marionette. The *beaux esprits* for whom the French are writing will never see the dawn of the rising day, for they do not believe in the resurrection of the flesh. No! Nature, to repeat, is Hebrew consonants from which the vowels are missing, an equation with at least one unknown, and we can fathom this unknown only by action, not by contemplation in accordance with rules.[1]

What kind of action? He speaks, as always, in metaphors. We must ravish nature, enter into and be at one with her: 'Nature is our old grandmother . . . to commit incest with this grandmother is the most important commandment of the Koran of the arts, and it is not obeyed.'[2] How can fastidious modern connoisseurs do this, since they are ashamed of nature, cover her up, concern themselves only with the pretty clothes with which they hide her?[3] Hamann's denunciations of the rationalists, and insistence on the wisdom that comes from true participation in life – at its highest level by the genius, at every level by human beings seeking to fulfil themselves – are perhaps the earliest hymn to the rejection of rules and norms and contemplation in favour of action. 'Think less and live more,'[4] he said to Herder – in that long line of the champions of life against

[1] B i 450.18. [2] w ii 342.28, 33. [3] w ii 347.8 ff.
[4] B ii 330.30.

99

what Goethe famously called 'grey theory',[1] which begins
in earnest with the German *Sturm und Drang*, from Heinse's
Ardinghello,[2] with its passionate call to throw away all convention and let all passions fulfil themselves, no matter how
destructively or how great the scandal to the respectable,
to Jacobi's *Allwill* and *Woldemar* (with its central doctrine
that 'What cannot be got wrong . . . has not much in it;
and what cannot be abused has little practical value'),[3] to
the cult of unbridled individualism of Schlegel's *Lucinde*,[4]
and continues towards Byron and Stirner and Nietzsche and
Hamsun and D. H. Lawrence.

'Every creature has a natural right to appropriate all that
surrounds it to the limits of its power'; these limits will be
determined only by the resistance of other creatures. All
calls to discipline are mere manifestations of 'bourgeois
order, which ruins man', just so much 'barbaric legislation'.[5] These doctrines of Heinse, which he admits may
seem wild, debauched, horrible to the mass of the philistine
public,[6] but will govern the lives of the truly free, who will
alone understand them, these are not the views of Hamann,
who believed in submission to the laws of God as we feel
them with our whole being; yet though he opposed the
general spirit of this cry for anarchy he admired the novel

[1] *Faust*, part 1, line 2038.

[2] Johann Jakob Wilhelm Heinse, *Ardinghello und die glückseeligen Inseln* (1787).

[3] *Eduard Allwills Papiere* (the titles of later revisions differ) was
published in 1775, *Woldemar* in 1779. The quotation from *Woldemar*
may be found in *Friedrich Heinrich Jacobi's Werke*, vol. 5 (Leipzig, 1820),
p. 113.

[4] Published in 1799.

[5] Wilhelm Heinse, *Ardinghello und die glückseeligen Inseln*, ed. Carl
Schüdderkopf (Leipzig, 1911) [vol. 4 of his edition of Heinse's *Sämmtliche Werke*], pp. 155, 111.

[6] Willhelm Körte (ed.), *Briefe zwischen Gleim, Wilhelm Heinse und
Johann von Müller* (Zürich, 1806), vol. 1 [*Briefe deutscher Gelehrten*, vol.
2], p. 123; cf. pp. 10, 55.

in which it was contained. '*Beauty is the appearance of our entire being unfalsified,*' said Heinse,[1] and this was Hamann's doctrine also. Beauty is life in its most characteristic, whole, dynamic, palpable form, full of conflict and contradiction as it may be – not smoothed out and brought to order by some theory-ridden Frenchman in a wig and silk stockings. This is the doctrine that he communicated to Herder, and that was destined to influence German romanticism, and through it all European thought.

He detested the tame imitations of this attitude more even than the materialism of the French. He disliked Sterne, for example, who was greatly admired by the romantics, because although he broke through the conventions and the rules, he took too much pleasure in his own waywardness, his attitude was too narcissistic, not passionate and single-minded enough, not serious, a mere pretence at unconventionality while remaining deeply embedded in the convention, a mild titillation of the philistine and the orthodox; and he equally detested the 'Anacreontic' poetry of Wieland and his disciples, pseudo-idyllic exercises, remoter from *actio* than the wrong-headed but formidable activity of, say, Voltaire, whose brilliance and verve Hamann admired as much as he condemned his doctrines.

The reader may enquire why Rousseau is not included in this catalogue of anti-intellectual naturalism. The reason is that Hamann's attitude to Rousseau, like that of many of the anti-rationalists, is exceedingly ambivalent. On the one hand *Émile* and *The Social Contract* are rationalist treatises with an artificial view of man worthy of Voltaire or Raynal or d'Alembert or the miserable Berlin rationalists, men who in the battle against fanaticism have themselves become rationalist fanatics, murderers, incendiaries, robbers, cheats of God and man. Rousseau is Utopian, a dabbler in abstractions; his theory of education is founded upon the absurd

[1] ibid., p. 255.

myth of 'beautiful nature, good taste and balanced reason';[1] school is not a peaceful harmony of teacher and pupil, as Rousseau would have it, but 'a mountain of God like Dothan, full of fiery chargers and chariots round Elisha'.[2] On the other hand there is a 'sensuous fascination'[3] in his novels greater than that of Richardson's, and his bitter indignation with the *salons* and convention, and his wish 'to serve men by his knowledge of the human heart acquired by his excesses and those of others',[4] are sympathetic. All this before he had read Rousseau's *Confessions*, before indeed these had appeared. And he had a kind word for Diderot, the most German among the French, who, in spite of his terrible rationalist views, realises that rules are not everything, that 'something more *immediate*, *intimate*, **obscure**, **certain**' is what matters.[5] Still, of course, Diderot follows a false philosophy – he occasionally repents of it, but is mostly in error. Hamann would have approved of Diderot's paean to genius (in a section of a *Salon* devoted to the painter Carle Van Loo) as something dark, farouche, unapproachable, as opposed to the twitter, the charm and sweetness, of the fashionable wits.[6] Yet Hamann is inconstant: he bursts forth with the most passionate admiration for *La Nouvelle Héloïse*, but later attacks it. Saint-Preux is an idiot and my Lord Edward is not an Englishman. Julie does not deserve love or admiration or the absurd sacrifice of these to the insupportable Wolmar: Rousseau's language is not that of the passions but of rhetoric. It is all false. It is all French.

Although Rousseau's tone, particularly in *La Nouvelle Héloïse* and the *Confessions*, is that of a free, rebellious spirit, what he advocates is the striking off of the old yoke – of convention or science or art – in order to impose anew one of those eternal laws which are graven within our hearts:

---

[1] w ii 356.26.   [2] w ii 356.16.   [3] B ii 104.19.
[4] B ii 105.22.   [5] B ii 84.11.
[6] Diderot, *Salon de 1765*, ed. Else Marie Bukdahl and Annette Lorenceau (Paris, 1984), p. 47.

the old morality preached by Plato and all the true sages of all times and climes. This is not what Hamann advocated. He wished to destroy what seemed to him the fixed, frozen establishment of rules and regulations as such, in order to reawaken in man a sense of his unity with God, and make him live spontaneously in him – if in a troubled relationship[1] – obedient to no rules that could be embodied in letters of any kind, ephemeral or eternal, least of all eternal. Hence Rousseau, in the end, was for him as Protagoras for Socrates, the best among the sophists, but still a sophist.

Goethe said of Hamann (to Chancellor Müller), 'He had a clear head in his day, and knew what he wanted,'[2] but Kant said 'The late Hamann had such a gift for thinking of things in general, but he did not have the power to point out their principles clearly, or at least to detach anything specific out of this wholesale trade of his.'[3] This is both amusing and true. But Hamann remained untouched by what he knew of Kant's attitude to him, and was, indeed, confirmed in his view of Kant as an intelligent man but blind – his eyes shut tightly against reality in order to perceive his own internal, imaginary structure more clearly. He would have echoed the romantic dramatist Klinger, who said 'Kant's iron Colossus of Rhodes – his imperative – or his fantastic touchstone swinging suspended over the moral world by a hair' was not a fit instrument by which to explain or judge mankind.[4] Hamann, who was not an altogether modest man, saw himself as a German Socrates, who refuses to engage in vain talk with the sophists,[5] and silences the

---

[1] w iii 312.36.

[2] Kanzler [Friedrich] von Müller, *Unterhaltungen mit Goethe*, ed. Ernst Grumach (Weimar, 1956), p. 99, 18 December 1823.

[3] See C. H. Gildemeister, *Johann Georg Hamann's, des Magus in Norden, Leben und Schriften*, vol. 6: *Hamann-Studien* (Gotha, 1873), p. 56.

[4] F. M. Klinger, *Betrachtungen und Gedanken über verschiedene Gegenstände der Welt und der Literatur*, § 55: p. 40 in *F. M. Klinger's Sämmtliche Werke*, vol. 11 (Stuttgart/Tübingen, 1842).

[5] w ii 73.2 ff.

importunate Athenians who pester him with too many questions, and gives his disciples courage to conquer their vanity by his example. His business was to blow up established values, both those of tradition and those of philosophy, and to organise a counter-revolution back towards simplicity and faith against the arrogance and optimism of the new science.

Socrates attempted to do his work by means of analytical reason. Hamann saw himself as doing so by other methods, by breaking through established conventions and expectations with every weapon that could break the crust of custom or dogma. This was the justification, in his own eyes, for his hermetic style, his mysterious formulae, with which he hoped to puzzle, intrigue and awaken the reader, his frenzied scurrying from one topic to another, his deliberately disordered succession of ideas, the constant self-incarnation in fantastic personages drawn from mythology or poetry or his own wild, extravagant imagination – anything to stop the reader in his tracks, harry him, astonish, irritate, open windows on new vistas; above all, to break the normal train of association to which his own unselfcritical life or the authority of his spiritual or literary guides had accustomed him. Into the reader thus awakened he hoped to pour the true word of God – the unity of spirit and flesh, the oneness of life, the need to live and create, the paramountcy of belief, the feebleness of reason, the fatal delusiveness of all contrived answers, constructed theories, everything calculated to lull the spirit into the false dream of reality. The true image of the practical man is that of a sleepwalker, a man who, with infinite sagacity, reflection, coherence, talks, acts, executes perilous enterprises, and does this with greater sureness of touch than he would – or could – do it if his eyes were even a little open.

This paradox is echoed by nearly every romantic writer – the confidence of the sleepwalker which comes from his blindness: reality is disturbing, but must be faced. The only way to awaken such deluded beings is by breaking the spectacles through which they normally look at reality, by affectation of madness, by the methods used later by Novalis, Hoffmann, Gogol, and in our own day by Pirandello, Kafka and the surrealists. Of course, only men of original genius can achieve this, and Hamann certainly believed himself to be one, no less than Socrates. Genius is not healthy, but a divine malady which, as Hippocrates says, is at once divine and human – *panta theia kai panta anthropina*[1] – that which unites heaven and earth. Genius is mad in the worldly sense, for the wisdom of this world is folly; and the only use of reason is not to give us knowledge but to expose to ourselves our own ignorance – to conduce to humility. That we have learnt from Socrates. But, as Hume correctly says, reason taken by itself is impotent, and when it dictates it is a usurper and an impostor.

This is Hamann's central message, and his own justification for his method. If it was a rationalisation of the fact – supposing it was a fact – that he was unable to write clearly because his thoughts were turbid and chaotic, the apologia is ingenious and had a powerful historical effect. Kant was properly horrified: 'One can only laugh', he said, at these 'men of genius, or perhaps apes of genius' – 'one can only laugh and continue on one's own path with assiduity, order, clarity, paying no attention to these jugglers'.[2] He was, no doubt, right. Nevertheless, it is doubtful whether without Hamann's revolt – or at any rate something similar – the worlds of Herder, Friedrich Schlegel, Tieck, Schiller, and indeed of Goethe too, would have come into being. Herder owed Hamann a great deal, and he and Jacobi – who owed him even more – were, with the brothers Schlegel, the chief subverters of the tradition of order,

[1] *On the Sacred Disease* xxi, (mis)quoted at w ii 105.24.
[2] Immanuel Kant, *Anthropologie in pragmatischer Hinsicht*, part 1, book 1, § 58: p. 226, line 10, in *Kant's gesammelte Schriften*, vol. 8 (Berlin, 1912).

rationalism, classicism, not only in Germany but in Europe. Madame de Staël's *De l'Allemagne* lifted the curtain on a part of this turbulence. The doctrines of Fichte and Schelling and even of Hegel, which strike the reader brought up in the Anglo-Saxon tradition of philosophy as wild irruptions into the well-ordered procession of sane and scrupulous rational European thinkers, could scarcely have taken place without this counter-revolution, which has cast alternate light and darkness upon the European scene, and, whether as cause or as symptom, is indissolubly connected with the most creative and the most destructive phenomena of our own time; this is the revolt of which Hamann was the first standard-bearer and perhaps the most original figure.

8   POLITICS

HAMANN'S POLITICAL views, such as they were, emerge most clearly, as always, in a protest against a particular position that irritated him: in this case one of Kant's best short essays, 'What is Enlightenment?' Kant's central thesis is that to be enlightened is to be responsible, even when obedience to legitimate authority is demanded, for one's own choices, to be independent, to determine oneself: not to allow others to lead one by the hand; not to be treated as a child, a minor, a ward. It is a passionate attack on paternalism, however benevolent, and a plea for individual freedom, equality and dignity, which Kant identifies with maturity and civilisation.

Hamann, of course, was outraged. Pride, independence, are the most fatal of all spiritual delusions. He protests, not of course against Kant's disapproval of childlike dependence on the part of subjects, but against his conception of the liberty of action due to truly enlightened men. Who has given the State, or its ruler and his hired professors, the right to tell others how to live? Who has certified them as ultimate authority – this self-appointed élite of sages and experts who have declared themselves infallible and presume to dictate to others? For him enlightenment and despotism – intellectual and political (for they are one) – march hand in hand. The *Aufklärung* is nothing but an aurora borealis – cold and illusory. He sees no good in the 'chatter' of those emancipated children (the philosophers) who constitute themselves guardians of the other guardians (the princes). All this rationalist patter seems to him like the cold light of the moon, which cannot be expected to illuminate our weak reason or warm our feeble will.[1] He looks for faith and finds it more readily among the untutored masses.

Hamann hated authorities, autocrats, self-appointed leaders – he was democratic and anti-liberal – and embodies one of the earliest combinations of populism and obscurantism, a genuine feeling for ordinary men and their values and the texture of their lives, joined with acute dislike for those who presume to tell them how to live. This kind of reactionary democracy, the union of anti-intellectualism and self-identification with the popular masses, is later to be found both in Cobbett and in the German nationalists of the Napoleonic wars, and is one of the strands that was most prominent in the Christian-Social Party in Austria, in the chauvinist clerical politics at the end of the century in France and, in due course, in Fascism and National Socialism, into which these streams in part poured themselves.

Yet Hamann does, with his customary penetration, point to the weakest parts of Kant's edifice. Kant, as a loyal Prussian subject, declared that if the prince or the sovereign orders me to do something that I deem to be wrong, I must as a private person – still more as an official – carry it out; I have no right to disobey; but as a rational being and member of a rational society I have a duty to criticise such an order. I am a combination: on the one hand a private person, on the other a publicist or philosopher or theologian or professor whose duty it is to speak out. Hamann does not think highly of this 'solution'. He asks whether, according to Kant, man is at once master and slave, guardian and minor, adult and not grown up. 'So the public use of reason and liberty is but a dessert, whereas the private use of these excellent things is the daily bread that we must give up, the better to taste the dessert.'[2] In public I wear the trappings of freedom, while at home I have nothing but

---

[1] B v 291.3 ff.   [2] B v 292.5.

the slave's rags? What is the use of this? Then he falls into his customary appeal to faith, for it alone gives us strength to resist the guardians and the tutors who not only kill our bodies but empty our pockets – faith, which is a concrete experience known to all, and not Kant's abstract 'good will', which is but an empty scholastic formula. Through it all he likes Kant; Kant is wrong-headed, hopelessly bemused by his own fantasies, but a decent old friend whose character one respects. It was a peculiar relationship.

Hamann admired Frederick the Great's greatness as a ruler, and his 'vital warmth'[1] as a man, but detested his policies and outlook, above all for putting reason, organisation and efficiency above humanity, God, variety, feeling; for creating a cold, elegant, magnificent, heartless social machine manipulated by logic-chopping sophists, *'political arithmeticians'*,[2] Frenchmen, Dutchmen and God knows what other imported dehumanised uniformed creatures; for despising Christianity, religion generally, for breaking up the old, intimate provincial Königsberg-Riga society. Hamann is the prophet Elijah and Frederick is the wicked king Ahab, whose subjects are corrupt and insolent and pagan and blasphemous and have starved and frozen the prophet almost to death. They have taken away five thalers a month from him, or at least the French administrator has – and this costs him his heating. The deduction is 'against all *rhyme* and *reason* – I am convinced that Your Majesty loves one and the other', he writes to him in the course of an appeal for justice.[3] Hamann is Jeremiah, he is the psalmist, he

---

[1] B vi 533.5.   [2] w iii 60.18.

[3] w iii 60.18. In another letter, to the Prussian General Administration (w ii 325–6), he begs for permission to take one afternoon off from his duties in order to sell his books, for otherwise he cannot survive. Elsewhere he begs for a job as a minor official in the Salt Tax Office, and to obtain the post but not the garden of his Dutch predecessor. When Hamann forced the lock, he was reprimanded, humiliated, crushed, driven into debt.

passes from curses and blessings to ponderous playfulness, indignation, melancholy, irony, prophetic fire. Let the King return to the Christian faith, let him dismiss his wicked, pagan Frenchmen, de Lattre and Guichard, who are eating his subjects' flesh. Frederick is Nero, he is Julian the Apostate,[1] again he is not Solomon, he is Ahab. The implication is that he treats Hamann as Ahab treated Naboth: he has taken away his *Hausrecht*.[2] Frederick is a philosophical anti-Christ who has taken the place of the Popish anti-Christ.[3] He has sold Prussia to a hollow cosmopolitan ideal, to foreigners, to sophists, lying prophets of this new Islam (perhaps Voltaire, perhaps a reference to Frederick himself). Hamann describes himself as one of 'les *petits* Philosophes de *grand-soucy*' as against 'les *grands* Philosophes *sans-soucy*'.[4] Tyrants and sophists are enemies of mankind: they place themselves above the herd of common men.[5] Then follows a passage which is a caricature of Herder's description of man as lord of creation *vis-à-vis* the beasts of the field. Frederick is the 'Solomon of Prussia'[6] and he understands well that there are two ways of government. 'One must either *coerce* or *deceive* one's subjects.'[7] But of course rulers must hide this fact – hence their hypocrisy. Only God can love *and* reign. Charity and authority cannot be combined on earth. To love subjects is to be their dupe, like the great God himself; or their victim, like his well-beloved Son.

[1] cf. w iii 145.9.

[2] There is something of the same sublimity of thought and miserable struggle for his salary and his rights in Giambattista Vico, in certain respects Hamann's forerunner: neither obtained his full due in his own century.

[3] B iv 260.26, in a letter to Herder dealing mostly with other matters; cf. Hamann's view that philosophy is '*popery* spiritualised by good sense' (w ii 290.36).

[4] w ii 319.19.   [5] cf. w ii 302.17.   [6] cf. p. 12 above.

[7] w ii 302.16. 'There are two ways of government,' said an eminent British statesman in the nineteenth century, in an unpublished conversation, 'bamboozle or bamboo.'

But if one is to gain resources in this world one must turn one's back on both charity and authority. Blood and gold – which alone rule the world – are the Devil's weapons. That is, so goes the implication, what Frederick and enlightened despots of his type accumulate.

His references to Frederick acquire a certain pitch of hysteria. Frederick is the head and leader of the conspiracy of reason against faith, in thought and in action. At times he speaks of his homosexuality in obscene language. Yet, of course, Hamann remains a loyal subject, a quietist, against resistance, in this respect like his friend Immanuel Kant, Prussian, Lutheran, obedient to all forms of *Obrigkeit*, anxious to avoid disorder. The subversive note comes not from the left but from the right, from the old, vanishing, domestic, narrowly provincial, semi-feudal Prussia as against the *Rechtsstaat* and the notion of a civilised world without frontiers. His extreme hatred of the new political ideal communicated itself to Herder, who perhaps did not need it. Both felt more tenderly towards the customs and songs of the primitive natives of the Baltic coast than towards the new, well-administered modern State, resting on the basis of uniform, clearly intelligible, impartial laws administered by well-trained, enlightened officials with little respect for tradition or the crooked alleys of the ancient, familiar Prussian establishment, its roots lost in pre-Roman times. There is nothing that Hamann or Herder detested so much as new brooms that swept clean, no matter what frightful accumulation of injustice and misery had built up beneath the ancient cobwebs of the traditional edifice.[1]

---

[1] This does not prevent Hamann from rebuking Frederick for pampering his pets at the expense of his subjects: 'It is not fitting to take the bread from the children and cast it to the little dogs.' W ii 293.20.

9 CONCLUSION

THERE IS much else that is of value in Hamann, and much absurdity too. His worship of Homer and Shakespeare is of little interest to us now, because this is a victory that he and his disciples have long won – though it was not as inevitable as it may now seem, if we remember not merely the notorious observations about Shakespeare by Voltaire, but the fact that the great French Encyclopaedia devoted no separate article to Homer, while Diderot's entry on Greek philosophy refers to him as 'a theologian, philosopher and poet'; it proceeds to quote the view of a 'well-known man' that he was unlikely to be read much in twenty years' time, although Diderot does protest that this 'shows a lack of philosophy and taste'.[1] Hamann read *Hamlet* with Herder, and although he does not say so, his references to his own lack of decision, stupidity, inability to cope with life, have led his interpreters to suppose that he partly identified himself with the Prince of Denmark. At the same time, there is no doubt that he saw himself as a genius and a prophet: Socrates was his only true predecessor.

An angel came down . . . and troubled the Well of Bethesda, in the five grottoes of which many who were sick, blind, lame, consumptive lay waiting for the waters to be stirred. So the genius must lower himself to destroy the rules, else the waters remain still; once the waters are troubled, a man must be the

---

[1] Diderot in the *Encyclopédie* (which also contains articles on the *Iliad* and the *Odyssey*), s.v. 'Grecs (philosophie des)', p. 908, col. 1.

first to step into them, if he wants to experience the virtue and effectiveness of the rules for himself.[1]

Good sense is the enemy: the sick, children and demigods cannot digest good sense, he told his great friend the pastor Lindner.[2] Lindner had asked him whether after all some rules were not needed to preserve order and decency, in art as in life; was not good sense, after all, the daily bread of philosophers and critics? Yes, he replied, 'infants need milk',[3] and human beings are, for these purposes, children looking up to their Heavenly Father, who as often as not astonishes them, hurls paradoxes at them, creates earthquakes, makes wars, and through the mouth of his chosen prophets says deeply upsetting things. Moses did not let the Children of Israel rest peacefully in the desert. Herder took great pleasure in describing Hamann's aesthetics as Mosaic. Hamann could speak to Herder, because Herder seemed to him childlike and to have a virginal soul like Virgil, while Kant was a frozen-up old pedant who understood nothing worth understanding. For Kant, the world – nature – is a dead, external object, to be observed, analysed, labelled; the relevant concepts and categories are to be properly examined, their connections established, and the great automaton that is the world for him can be described and explained by a cut and dried system which, if it is true at all, will remain true for ever. No doubt this is an improvement on the cruder mechanistic views of the French materialists, but the presuppositions are the same: that a series of logically interconnected propositions of a descriptive kind can account for everything, and that conduct and the vast universe of men, beasts, material objects, life, soul, heaven and earth can be classified and interpreted in terms of one systematic unifying instrument – the correct theory, something that any man, provided he is impartial enough, able

[1] w ii 362.1.   [2] w ii 361.1 ff.   [3] w ii 361.3.

enough, and sets himself to it, can invent or at any rate understand.

All his life Hamann struggled violently to deny and expose this. His doctrines and his style reflect each other and his view of the world as an unorderable succession of episodes, each carrying its value in itself, intelligible only by direct experience, a 'living through' this experience, unintelligible – dead – when it is reported by others. A man must live on his own account, not as a pensioner of others, and to 'live on one's own account' is to report – or, as often as not, fail to report – what one has lived through, and to use theories only as crutches to be thrown away when direct experience presents itself. No complete account of anything can be achieved by these means. Kant has rightly won the day, but Hamann and his followers express a continual revolt against taking so much so blandly for granted, against leaving out so much, perhaps necessarily, but with too little regret, with no qualms, as if what the theory cannot embrace is mere expendable rubbish: psychological idiosyncrasy, oddities and quirks, which the theory cannot notice and which in a rational universe will themselves be ironed out, so that the facts will be only such as the final infallible theory fits.

Hamann sees the same all-conquering monism in the Roman Church and in the dream of a universal science as preached by the French Encyclopaedia; this seems to him to ignore and obliterate differences in thought and feeling, and to sweep them aside in practice. He fears system, centralisation, monism, as such, and his view of the authoritative role demanded by the sciences of his day as something of a secular version of the claims of the Catholic hierarchy is echoed in the following century by Auguste Comte – save that this was an object of horror to Hamann and of complete approval to Comte. Hamann saw in this convergence yet another example of the 'coincidence of opposites', a doctrine originated by Nicholas of Cusa (Hamann mistakenly ascribed it to Giordano Bruno) – although it is not clear how far he understood it, and he certainly gives it a sense of his own. Nevertheless, this war on two fronts against the conflicting claims to all knowledge – of the Church on the right and of science on the left – is a position of which Hamann is perhaps the most single-minded and passionate, as well as the earliest, representative – and with which he imbued the romantics and after them the individualist liberals of the nineteenth century. When Herzen speaks of communism (of such writers as Cabet or the Babouvists) as simply tsarism stood on its head, an equally oppressive and individuality-ignoring system, and when Bakunin complains of Marx's authoritarianism, this is the tradition they continue – the terror of any establishment that hems in the individual and destroys his deepest values.

Hamann, in a very characteristic phrase, already quoted, summarises this in saying of Descartes' 'Cogito ergo sum', it is all very well about the *cogito* (that is, rationalism), but what about the 'noble *sum*'?[1] Any doctrine that stresses the general, the impersonal, the conceptual, the universal, seems to him likely to flatten out all differences, peculiarities, quirks – to obstruct the soul's free flight by clipping its wings in the interests of comprehensive inclusiveness. The ambition to 'Newtonise' all knowledge tends to work against sensitiveness to each fleeting particular, to lower susceptibility to empirical impressions – to stress form at the expense of content, uniformity at the expense of variety, fullness of life, the kaleidoscopic metamorphoses of actual experience that slip through the meshes of the most elaborate conceptual net. Like William James more than a century later, Hamann is a champion of the individual, the complex and above all the unconscious and the unseizable. Far more than James, he defends the inarticulate, the mystical, the demonic, the dark reaches and mysterious depths.

[1] B vi 230.35; cf. p. 59 above, note 6.

Virtue and philanthropy are no substitute for compassion, love, generosity of spirit. Hamann reacted against the bland neglect of the animal and diabolical element in men on the part of the eighteenth-century optimists and naturalists, and when Kant, in the first part of *The Philosophical Doctrine of Religion*, speaks of radical evil and calls for a rebirth – something that even Herder, let alone Goethe and Schiller, was remote from – Hamann understands this only too well. 'The defects and the holes – that is the deepest and highest knowledge of human nature, whereby alone man can rise to the ideal',[1] and 'nothing but the descent to hell [*Höllenfahrt*] of self-knowledge builds the path to becoming divine [*Vergötterung*]':[2] this is quoted by Kant.[3]

Hence also Hamann's passionate defence of freedom of the will:

> Without freedom to be *wicked*, there is no *merit*, and without freedom to be *good*, no attribution of any *guilt*, indeed no *knowledge of good and evil* at all. Freedom is the *maximum* and *minimum* of all our natural powers, both the base and the goal of their entire direction, development and return.
>
> Neither *instinct* nor *sensus communis* determines *man* . . . Each man is his own *lawgiver*, but also the *first-born* and *most immediate* of his *subjects*.[4]

Only indeterminism can explain the spiritual development of the human race, since without 'the law of freedom' man would be nothing but an imitator; 'for man is of all the animals the greatest *mime*'.[5] He believed this politically, morally and in the sphere of self-knowledge also.

The fear of monism in all its forms – whether as the comprehensive scientific treatise or centralised religious or political establishment – is usually the cry of a trapped man

---

[1] B iii 34.33.   [2] w ii 164.17.
[3] *Kant's gesammelte Schriften*, vol. 7 (Berlin, 1907), p. 55.
[4] w iii 38.8.   [5] w iii 38.20.

(or class) who cannot be brought to see that to be regimented or eliminated is either inevitable or desirable; the idea he or others cling to may be unsatisfactory or even detestable, but to be torn away from it must evoke a cry of pain and despair. It may be that the old ways of life are to be condemned. Montesquieu cautiously advocates care and slowness in making changes because he thinks that the kind of radical reforms that even in his day men began to demand would be ineffective or too despotic. Hamann condemns monism because all generalisation for him embodies false values. Tom Paine accused Burke, who uttered conservative sentiments in his attack on the French Revolution, of admiring the plumage while ignoring the dying bird. Hamann is not guilty of Burke's particular form of complacency. Nevertheless, he too, in his own way, is blind to the cry of human misery, unless it is of an individual or spiritual character. Those who put an end to suttee, or cleared slums, or created tolerable conditions of life in the place of some crushing, poverty-stricken patriarchalism, have rightly not been condemned by the majority of mankind. Hamann speaks for those who hear the cry of the toad beneath the harrow, even when it may be right to plough over him: since if men do not hear this cry, if they are deaf, if the toad is written off because he has been 'condemned by history' – if the defeated are never worth attending to because history is the history of the victorious – then such victories will prove their own undoing, for they will tend to destroy the very values in the name of which the battle was undertaken. The cry from the heart of human beings pushed against the wall by Frederick's great new broom, which swept so clean, and in a sense so permanently, is what is heard in all Hamann's writings. He spoke for ultimate human values no less than did his enlightened opponents, Voltaire and Kant, who are rightly admired as defenders of human rights.

*

Hamann knows that not one reader in a hundred will understand his writings, but he begs, with a curious mixture of pathos and arrogance, that he be accorded the treatment accorded to Heraclitus by Socrates: who, it is said, believed the passages that he could not understand because of the great value of those that he did. He compares his own prose to an archipelago of isolated islands; he cannot throw bridges across them, for that is precisely what he is against, the construction of a system that obliterates what is most living, individual, real. The vision that obsessed him was that of a world in process of perpetual re-creation, a process that cannot be stopped. It has to be described in what are inevitably static terms. It is not a slow growth – Hamann is not a historicist; he does not believe, or at least is not interested, in development. For him the world grows neither better nor worse. But there is an original, transcendent pattern, as it were, of which everything is a reflection or an analogy or an intimation. In the Garden of Eden, before the expulsion from Paradise, Adam was acquainted with it: 'Adam was of God, and God himself brought in the oldest of our race so that he might possess in fief and heritage the world, and the world be fulfilled by the word of his mouth.'[1]

> Every phenomenon of nature was a name – the sign, the symbol, the promise of a fresh and secret and ineffable but all the more intimate chosen union, communication and communion of divine energies and ideas. All that man in these beginnings heard with his ears, saw with his eyes, contemplated or touched with his hands, all this was the living word. For God was the Word. With the Word in his mouth and in his heart, the origin of language was as natural, as near and as easy as a child's play.[2]

This dark and mystical passage, already quoted in connec-

[1] W iii 32.8. [2] W iii 32.21.

tion with Hamann's views of language, is the nearest that we can get to the central vision. It is one in which Hamann conceives the unity of thought and object – which he calls word and world – as mystics and metaphysicians have often conceived it: the unbroken unity of thought and feeling, not yet of immediacy and knowledge, not yet broken into subject and object, the knower and the known, which man is perpetually attempting to transcend. Whoever, whenever and wherever they may be, men, according to Hamann, have a choice of two alternatives. The first is to seek truly to understand, which means to perceive what this primal pattern may be as well as they are able (although they can never see it all, being finite) through direct experience, whether of history or of nature, or by reading the words of the Bible, which is an attempt of the unity to express itself in language intelligible to finite men; the second alternative is to shield oneself from reality by the construction of systems, by belief in conventional institutions, by living life according to the dictates of good sense. 'Three things . . . I cannot comprehend, possibly four: a *man of sound judgement* who looks for the philosophers' stone; the squaring of a circle; the extent of the sea; and a *man of genius* who *affects the religion of sound human reason.*'[1] God is a poet: the world is an act of perpetual creation in accordance with a pattern that cannot be reduced to rules, which can only be perceived by the reflection that each of God's creations is another thing – by the fact that all events and objects are themselves, but are also symbols of, hieroglyphs of, allusions to, throw light upon, every other thing.

Quite apart from the intrinsic value of this profoundly irrationalist spiritual vision, its importance in the history of ideas (and of practice) is as a glove thrown down against the claim of the sciences, whether empirical or a priori, to answer all the central human questions. Hamann in the end

---

[1] w ii 294.6.

recognises only the individual and his temperament, and he thinks that all attempts to generalise lead to the creation of faceless abstractions that are then taken for the individuals who are the raw material for the abstractions, with the consequence that theories propounded in terms of these abstractions do not touch the core of the individuals whom they purport to describe or explain, and the legal, moral and aesthetic systems – every formulation of principles of action – either ignore the individuals from whose experience they are in the end drawn, or force them into some Procrustean bed of conformity to rules which certainly maim and may destroy them.

When Hamann inveighs against all abstraction, if what he says is taken literally it is pure nonsense. Without some generalisation there can be no symbols, no words, no thought. Wherever anything is used to stand for anything else – Hamann's favourite and most original field of speculation – some degree of generalisation occurs of whatever is used as a symbol: it is removed from its natural medium, whatever that may be, and made to stand for something else, in order to discriminate this something else from other things similar or dissimilar to it, so that both the symbol and the symbolised, if they are to be identified at all, can only be so by means of general terms. To forbid abstraction is to forbid thought, self-consciousness, articulation of any kind; to confine the agent to sensation and musing and dreams, whether by day or by night, with no power of naming them. Hamann certainly did not mean this, but he occasionally speaks as if he did; and his denunciation of the sciences, which carry abstraction beyond common speech, turns into a denial of their necessary function in their own field, into an attack on thought as such, as opposed to sensation or the mystery of artistic creation.

The distinction that Hamann seeks to establish between abstract thought and concrete certainty is, as it stands, illicit, and when driven as far as he drives it turns into blind obscurantism, an attack on critical thought, the making of distinctions, the formulation of hypotheses, ratiocination itself, an onslaught which springs from anger and hatred of criticism and, in the end, all mental activity. But despite the fact that Hamann's words are often passionate rhetoric and not careful thought, his general trend is not obscure. Like Burke some years later, he thinks that the application of scientific canons to living human beings leads to an erroneous and ultimately a deeply degrading view of what they are — mere human material, a field for physical, chemical and biological causation — and, since nobody was ever more acutely conscious of the unity of theory and practice, an inhuman attitude towards men. The fact that an equal, if not a greater, degree of inhumanity was practised by those who rejected science and allowed men to live in remediable poverty, ignorance and oppression left him unaffected. Often men can see clearly out of only one window.

Hamann was a fanatic, and his vision of life, despite its sincerity and depth and the value that believers in God and theologians have perceived in it, is, as a general philosophy of life, grotesquely one-sided: a violent exaggeration of the uniqueness of men and things, or the absence in them of significant common characteristics capable of being abstracted and theorised about; a passionate hatred of men's wish to understand the universe or themselves in publicly intelligible terms and to rule themselves and nature in order to achieve ends common to most men at most times (to go no further) by taking such scientific knowledge into account. This hatred and this blind irrationalism have fed the stream that has led to social and political irrationalism, particularly in Germany, in our own century, and has made for obscurantism, a revelling in darkness, the discrediting of that appeal to rational discussion in terms of principles intelligible to most men which alone can lead to an increase of knowledge, the creation of conditions for free co-operative action based on conscious acceptance of common ideals, and the promotion of the only type of progress that has ever deserved this name.

The importance of Hamann consists not in his bitterly obscurantist particularism and denigration of systematic thought and of the demand that actions be accountable in terms of freely and openly debatable principles, even though that was his own constant practice, as in his polemics with Kant; it lies in the inspired insights which this uncommonly sensitive and painfully candid man achieved into those aspects of human life which the sciences are apt to ignore — perhaps must ignore, because of their very nature as sciences. His cry came from an outraged sensibility: he spoke as a man of feeling offended by a passion for a cerebral approach; as a moralist who understood that ethics is concerned with relations between real persons (under God as the ultimate ruler whose will they try to obey as his servants); as a man who was offended by the enunciation of principles that claimed a pseudo-scientific objectivity not derived from individual or social experience; as a German humiliated by an arrogant and, it seemed to him, spiritually blind West; as a humble member of a dying social order, trampled by the inhuman tempo of centralisation in the political and cultural sphere. Forced by arrogant dictators, Frederick and Voltaire, he rose in rebellion and instituted a fierce campaign against reason. Nevertheless, as with most rebellions, there was real oppression to fight against — in this case, a suppression of individuality and irrational and unconscious forces in men which sooner or later was bound to provoke an explosion. Hamann, while apparently engaged in confused and incomprehensible theological tracts, lit a fuse — I know of no one earlier or more directly responsible for this (although who can tell whether without him the course of human history, or even thought in Germany, would have been very different?) — which set off the great romantic revolt, the denial that there was an objective order, a *rerum natura*, whether factual or normative, from which all knowledge and all values stemmed, and by which all action could be tested.

The revolution began in Germany — perhaps for political reasons which inhibited social and political agitation, and indeed open discussion, and forced criticism into what Alexander Herzen once called the 'tranquil sea of aesthetic theory'.[1] At the centre of it were: the identity of language and thought; the idea of art as neither imitation of an ideal beauty, objectively accessible to all men, nor a means of giving pleasure governed by rules open to anyone to verify; the combination of a Humean empiricism that killed the authority of a priori principles with an emphasis on the supreme value of individual self-expression; the unique working of God in each sentient spirit in its own inexplicable way, not necessarily reconcilable with that at work in any other. All this proved a violently explosive amalgam which, whether or not it was itself a consequence of social or economic tensions, proved to be a great and world-transforming power with all the terrifying consequences that Heine, almost alone among writers before our own century, so accurately prophesied when he warned the French not to underestimate the power of the quiet German philosopher in his study. If Hamann had not enunciated, in however peculiar a fashion, truths too contemptuously ignored by the triumphant rationalist schools, not only in his own century, but in the great Victorian advance and its continuation in countries that came relatively late to this feast of reason, the movement that he initiated would not have had its formidable consequences on both thought and action, not least in our own terrible century. This is sufficient reason for rescuing his memory from the pages of purely literary or theological specialists.

One has only to compare the attempts to rebut the doctrines of the Enlightenment made by the official apologists

---

[1] *Sobranie sochinenii v tridtsati tomakh*, vol. 9 (Moscow, 1956), p. 21.

of the Churches on the one hand, and the attempts at compromise made by Hamann's *bêtes noires*, the liberal theologians, on the other hand, to realise the full extent of Hamann's originality. On the side of the Sorbonne and the Catholic opposition one finds, for the most part, either blind dogmatism together with eccentric denials of the reliability of scientific or historical investigation in their own fields, or feeble efforts to show that what the *philosophes* claim to do, the Church – in its slow but nevertheless rational fashion – can do better. Apart from organised opposition of this type, there were the Protestant sects and movements which protected themselves against rationalism by attitudes of hostile indifference, 'know-nothing' parties which turned towards inward meditation and holy living, opting out of the social and political world either voluntarily or because of political barriers. This left the spiritual opposition to the march of reason to the illuminist and Masonic lodges, which even in the writings of their most influential and distinguished representatives, such as, for example, Saint-Martin, were incomparably less original or concerned with the critical issues – either individual or social – than even Hamann's darkest and most eccentric pieces. His central charge, that writers claiming to understand man and nature by direct observation ignore the areas of life that are closest to them in their daily experience – the actual way in which men act and what they believe – and the justice, and poignant and uncompromising audacity, with which he plunges the knife into those wounds which were duly uncovered for all to see in the decades that followed his death, give him his unique importance in the history of thought.

Hamann was not a nostalgic medievalist who contrasted an imaginary past, seen as a better and nobler age, with the dreary mediocrity of the present. His fantasies were timeless and not historical. But like the later denouncers of industrial civilisation, he steadfastly ignored not merely the causes but the purposes of the secular reformers. The application of rational methods to social policy, whether in Frederick's Prussia or Napoleonic France or even Joseph II's Holy Roman Empire, had as its purpose the removal of glaring injustices and irrational conflicts, human misery and oppression; and its achievements form a bright page in an otherwise none too brilliant portion of human history. The very notions of progress and reaction were born in the course of the conflict between, on the one hand, those who desired to introduce rapid changes (in the course of which they overestimated their own power and the malleability of men, and made empirical errors which caused much unnecessary suffering) and, on the other, those who for one reason or another – whether because of the interests of their class or nation, or because the Utopianism of the reformers struck them as at once shallow and insane – resisted.

Hamann belonged to the latter category. The world that the reformers were seeking to build seemed to him a denial of all the values that he prized and that he believed to be most deeply embedded in the nature of men. Because this was so, he remained blind to the worst abuses of the regime in which he lived: he saw only the vices of the 'great simplifiers' who were seeking to destroy living men and women in the name of hollow abstractions – ideals like reason, progress, liberty or equality, vast, balloon-like constructions of unrealistic minds – all of which taken together were worth less than acquaintance with one concrete fact, one real human being, one hour in the true, that is inner, experience of one human soul and one human body, as they really were in all their painful imperfection.

The contrasts and conflicts between the categories of quantity and quality have been familiar for a long while and have taken many forms – aesthetic, ethical, political, logical. This is indeed, in its sociological form, still one of the most profound issues that dominates the attitudes of men. But in Hamann's day it was a relatively new issue.

The possibility of applying quantitative generalisations not only to the physical world – there the battle had been won in the seventeenth century – but to social and personal life as well – in the organisation of life on scientific principles, the calculation of relative sums of satisfaction between human beings conceived as equal (or if unequal, with the inequalities reducible to some common standard of measurement) – was prophesied with enthusiasm by Condorcet. Quantification, verification of numerically statable hypotheses, and planning on this basis, whether for individuals or for groups or for larger bodies of human beings, had scarcely entered their first stage. If anything is destined to be selected as characteristic of the new age that began in the seventeenth century, it is the transition from qualitative to quantitative concepts that laid the foundation not merely of physics and biology but of all the social sciences and the moral and economic outlook associated with this, together with its by-products in ethics and aesthetics.

All this is by now a truism. To repeat myself: one of Hamann's greatest claims to our notice is that, earlier than any other thinker, he became conscious of this, and protested violently. If to attempt to resist the swelling current of thought of an age and a civilisation is to be reactionary, then certainly Hamann was a complete and vehement reactionary. He knew this, and gloried in it. He spoke out, in his cryptic but violent fashion, a quarter of a century before Burke uttered his famous lament for the passing of the age of chivalry and the arrival of the sordid mechanical men with their slide-rules and statistical tables.[1] After the great revolution in France, and when the consequences of the industrial revolution in England penetrated every sphere of

---

[1] 'But the age of chivalry is gone. – That of sophisters, oeconomists, and calculators, has succeeded; and the glory of Europe is extinguished for ever.' Edmund Burke, *Reflections on the Revolution in France* (1790): p. 127 in *The Writings and Speeches of Edmund Burke*, vol. 8, *The French Revolution*, ed. L. G. Mitchell (Oxford, 1979).

life, the conservative reaction of men like Chateaubriand or Maistre or Coleridge or Friedrich Schlegel or Novalis was to be expected. Hamann belongs to the small class of acutely sensitive persons with the gift – or the misfortune – of divining the contours of the future, whether to welcome them or recoil, as he did, in fear and hostility. Such men as a rule scarcely have the vocabulary in which to express something that resembles feeling more than an articulated vision; nevertheless, being poets (whose naturally responsive – irritable – constitutions are the first to react to such profound changes in human life), they find words, however obscure and charged with subjective emotion, to express their sense of the approaching cataclysm. Such men are justly called prophets, and, whether they know it or not, are gifted with a historical sense beyond the usual degree. When they come too early, it is difficult for them to convey the sense of what they feel in every pore of their being to men with a more normal vision. To see what others cannot see as yet, particularly if it appears as the sure sign of an approaching doom, and to be unable not to speak, drives such living divining-rods into themselves or into escape to some province free from the darkening world in which they are compelled to live. It may be that members of backward communities on the edges of a culture that is being radically transformed, who at once feel powerless to alter the current and are tied more deeply to the older culture that is being displaced, are peculiarly sensitive to such change: Naples at the turn of the seventeenth century, and Königsberg half a century later, were not at the centre of events, either politically or intellectually. At any rate, an explanation in sociological terms – which was something that all his life Hamann resisted as a false interpretation of history – fits his case. The type of household in which he was brought up, the life lived by the Inspector of Baths, as his father was proud to be described, was being crushed out of existence by the reforms of Frederick and his genuinely enlightened administrators. The son never found a secure place in the new establishment, and like many men who conceive bold ideas and speak in fierce and sweeping terms, was himself timid, gentle, self-distrustful and exceptionally vulnerable. Despite the calm and serene advice that he gave to other troubled spirits to cease from fretting, to surrender themselves wholly to God, to eat their bread and drink their wine in contentment, he himself nearly went out of his mind when his salary was reduced by five thalers and the size of his garden was cut down. He struck the first blow against the quantified world; his attack was often ill-judged, but he raised some of the greatest issues of our times by refusing to accept their advent.

APPENDIX

I ALLUDED above to the success in our own day of a theory of language like Hamann's; and to the odd combination of his view of language with his religious devotion and irrationalism.[1] A few more words may be said on these subjects.

Hamann in effect maintained the following:

(*a*) There is no objective 'structure' of reality of which a 'logically perfect language' would be the correct reflection.

(*b*) Propositions for which philosophers have claimed universal validity are therefore necessarily hollow.

(*c*) Rules and laws hold while they hold, but when they do not, they must be broken.

(*d*) Problems in theory (and mistakes in practice) are generated not by mistakes in logical or metaphysical or psychological theory so much as by fanatical belief in the universal and eternal validity of theories as such – by the belief that, if not this theory, then some other one will answer all our questions (even within a given sphere). It is this addiction to theory, and in particular to scientific theories, that breeds imaginary entities which are confounded with things in real life, and leads to mental confusions, and, at times, spiritual torments, due to an obstinate adherence to man-made figments that springs in its turn from the quest for universality – a philosophers' stone, as Hamann called this wish.

[1] See p. 91.

(*e*) Every language is a way of life, and a way of life is based on a pattern of experience which cannot itself be subjected to criticism, since one cannot find an Archimedean point outside it from which to conduct such a critical examination; at most, all one can do is to examine the symbolism by which the pattern of experience is expressed. This is so because to think is to use symbols, and as the symbols so the thought. Above all, content and form cannot be divorced – there is an 'organic' connection between all the elements of a medium of communication, and the meaning lies in the individual, ultimately unanalysable, whole.

(*f*) Perfect translation between different vocabularies, grammars, etymologies, syntaxes is in principle impossible, and the quest for a universal language, from which the irrational accretions and individual idiosyncrasies of natural languages would be cleansed – for instance Leibniz's belief in the possibility of this (called by him the 'Universal Characteristic'), or the universal language of science, which would respond to all human needs, dreamt of by Condorcet, and after him by many positivist thinkers – is the most absurd chimera of all.

(*g*) A corollary of (*f*): one cannot truly understand what men are saying by merely applying grammatical or logical or any other kind of rules, but only by an act of 'entering into' – what Herder called 'Einfühlung' – their symbolisms, and for that reason only by the preservation of actual usage, past and present. Even dialects and jargons – in so far as these bear 'the stamp of life' – are at the heart of ways of living and creating which uniformity in language, by producing uniformity in life, would destroy.

(*h*) Consequently, while we cannot do without rules and principles, we must constantly distrust them and never be betrayed by them into rejecting or ignoring or riding roughshod over the irregularities and peculiarities offered by concrete experience.

This is surely a doctrine that was not wholly unfamiliar in the middle of our century among English-speaking philosophers.

If this conception of language and meaning is valid, it follows that there are no ethical, aesthetic, ideological, social or religious beliefs that are excluded. Yet another thing follows. Since all thought and speech for Hamann is communication, it must be communication between specific individuals. But if these individuals are to understand each other as fully as life on earth permits they must enter into the individual images and texture that are indissoluble from the specific content of what a man is saying or, if he is an artist, making. To ask for words or works of art that will be intelligible to anyone anywhere is as absurd as the quest for the universal language. The worst of all standards is that of *bon sens*, that universal human good sense of which Descartes had spoken approvingly and which to Hamann is a guarantee of shallowness, philistinism and the all-flattening power that reduces everything to equal triviality. Hence his defence of the esoteric as such. This may indeed have been an attempt to justify his own passion to remain mysterious, to speak only to the few who could understand him – but he generalises it into a doctrine according to which all art, all creation, is a mystery which by being given rules and made public is distorted and degraded: this is the crime of the ancient Greeks and the modern French, who have turned this profoundly private, individual and at times terrifying process into a mechanised craft that anyone may perform and anyone respond to, save that both activities would be deprived of value.

All his life Hamann had a certain taste for mystagogues, even when he knew them to be charlatans, like the 'prophet' Christoph Kaufmann in his goatskin who shocked and intrigued the citizens of Königsberg and with whom Hamann entered into an ambivalent but fascinated relationship. Hamann represented himself, not unwillingly, as a dispenser of secret wisdom, a man not intending fully to be understood, an ironical Socrates, a Rosicrucian knight, an 'apocryphal' sibyl and the like. Though he never expressed it in these terms, he wished to be a teacher of wisdom, a sage, a guru, a rescuer of the unfortunate victims caught in the great net of the Enlightenment.

BIBLIOGRAPHICAL NOTE

THE STANDARD complete editions of Hamann's writings are
these:

Works: Johann Georg Hamann, *Sämtliche Werke*, ed. Joseph
    Nadler (Vienna, 1949–57: Herder), 6 vols. The last vol-
    ume contains an invaluable analytical index.
Letters: Johann Georg Hamann, *Briefwechsel*, ed. Walther
    Ziesemer and Arthur Henkel (Wiesbaden and Frankfurt,
    1955–79: Insel), 6 vols. Unfortunately there is not yet
    an index to these volumes, though one is in preparation.

In the references to Hamann's writings given in the footnotes to this book, these editions are referred to as W and
B respectively, and passages are cited by volume, page and
first line, thus: W iii 145.13.

Readers who do not (easily) read German may be glad to
have details of the few translations into English of Hamann's
writings. I cannot claim that I have discovered them all,
but details follow of the ones I have encountered in my
work on Isaiah Berlin's text. I should add for readers of
French that the second volume of Nadler's edition of Hamann's works contains most of the few pieces he wrote in
that language (there is also one in the third volume).

Aesthetica in nuce {Aesthetics in a Nutshell}: A Rhapsody in Cab-
    balistic Prose, trans. Joyce P. Crick, in H. B. Nisbet (ed.),
    German Aesthetic and Literary Criticism: Winckelmann, Less-
    ing, Hamann, Herder, Schiller, Goethe (Cambridge etc.,

1985: Cambridge University Press), pp. 139–50, notes pp. 275–86.

Golgotha and Scheblimini!, trans. Stephen N. Dunning in his *The Tongues of Men: Hegel and Hamann on Religious Language and History* (Missoula, 1979: Scholars Press), pp. 209–28, notes p. 247.

Hamann's 'Socratic Memorabilia': A Translation and Commentary, by James C. O'Flaherty (Baltimore, 1967: Johns Hopkins Press).

Letter to Kant, 27 July 1759, in *Kant: Philosophical Correspondence 1759–99*, ed. and trans. Arnulf Zweig (Chicago and London, 1967: University of Chicago Press), pp. 35–43.

'The Merchant' (an anonymous translation of all but the opening and closing pages of Hamann's supplement to his translation of Plumard de Dangeul's *Remarques sur les avantages et les désavantages de la France et de la Gr. Bretagne, par rapport au commerce, & aux autres sources de la puissance des états*), in Frederic H. Hedge (ed.), *Prose Writers of Germany* (Philadelphia, 1848), pp. 121–7.

Selections in Ronald Gregor Smith, *J. G. Hamann 1730–1788: A Study in Christian Existence, with Selections from his Writings* (London, 1960: Collins). Much of what is translated in this volume takes the form of extracts, but there are also several complete items, viz.: *Fragments*; *The Wise Men from the East in Bethlehem*; *New Apology of the Letter H by Itself*; review of Kant's *Critique of Pure Reason*; *Metacritique*.

There are also a few other books on Hamann in English known to me, which I list here. Their bibliographies may be consulted for details of articles in English, and of the growing literature in other languages.

W. M. Alexander, *Johann Georg Hamann: Philosophy and Faith* (The Hague, 1966: Martinus Nijhoff).

Terence J. German, *Hamann on Language and Religion* (Oxford, 1981: Oxford University Press).

Walter Leibrecht, *God and Man in the Thought of Hamann*, trans. James H. Stam and Martin H. Bertram (Philadelphia, 1966: Fortress Press) [original German edition 1958].

Walter Lowrie, *Johann Georg Hamann: An Existentialist* (Princeton, 1950: Princeton Theological Seminary).

James C. O'Flaherty, *Unity and Language: A Study in the Philosophy of Johann Georg Hamann* (Chapel Hill, 1952: University of North Carolina; New York, 1966: AMS Press).

James C. O'Flaherty, *Johann Georg Hamann* (Boston, 1979: Twayne).

Larry Vaughan, *Johann Georg Hamann: Metaphysics of Language and Vision of History* (New York etc., 1989: Peter Lang).

H.H.

INDEX

Compiled by Douglas Matthews